Muay Thai Counter Techniques
Competitive Skills and Tactics for Success

Christoph Delp

BLUE SNAKE BOOKS
BERKELEY, CALIFORNIA

Copyright © 2004, 2013 by Christoph Delp. All rights reserved. No portion of this book, except for brief review, may be reproduced, stored in a retrieval system, or transmitted in any form or by any means—electronic, mechanical, photocopying, recording, or otherwise—without written permission of the publisher. For information contact Blue Snake Books c/o North Atlantic Books.

Published by Blue Snake Books, an imprint of North Atlantic Books
P.O. Box 12327
Berkeley, California 94712

The first edition of this book was published by Frog, Ltd. in 2004 as *Muay Thai: Advanced Kickboxing Techniques*.

Cover photo by Nopphadol Viwatkamolwat
Cover and book design by Brad Greene
Printed in the United States of America

Muay Thai Counter Techniques: Competitive Skills and Tactics for Success is sponsored by the Society for the Study of Native Arts and Sciences, a nonprofit educational corporation whose goals are to develop an educational and cross-cultural perspective linking various scientific, social, and artistic fields; to nurture a holistic view of arts, sciences, humanities, and healing; and to publish and distribute literature on the relationship of mind, body, and nature.

> North Atlantic Books' publications are available through most bookstores. For further information, call 800-733-3000 or visit our websites at www.northatlanticbooks.com and www.bluesnakebooks.com.

PLEASE NOTE: The author, creators, and publishers of this book disclaim any liabilities for loss in connection with following any of the practices, exercises, and advice contained herein. To reduce the chance of injury or any other harm, the reader should consult a professional before undertaking this or any other martial arts, movement, meditative arts, health, or exercise program. The instructions and advice printed in this book are not in any way intended as a substitute for medical, mental, or emotional counseling with a licensed physician or healthcare provider.

Library of Congress Cataloging-in-Publication Data

Delp, Christoph, 1974–
 [Thaiboxen fight. English.]
 Muay Thai counter techniques : competitive skills and tactics for success / Christoph Delp.
   p. cm.
 Includes bibliographical references.
 Summary: "Designed for intermediate and advanced Muay Thai and Mixed Martial Arts fighters as well as their trainers"—Provided by publisher.
 ISBN 978-1-58394-543-8
 1. Muay Thai—Thailand. 2. Mixed martial arts. I. Title.
 GV1127.T45D4613 2012
 796.815—dc23
                    2012023264

1 2 3 4 5 6 7 8 9 VERSA 18 17 16 15 14 13

Paruehatnoi Sitjamee hits Yordradaap Daopaedrew with a kick.
Lumpinee Stadium, Bangkok, 2001.

Muay Thai

Muay Thai fights are spectacular, thrilling, and captivating. The athletes fight with dedication and passion, carrying themselves through to exhaustion.

Muay Thai is a martial art with an impressive variety of techniques. All the opponent's attacking techniques can be countered by a large number of moves. No two fighters act the same way because on the basis of basic techniques, fighters learn a range of further techniques and adapt these to their individual fighting style. For improvement, the athletes continue supplementing their repertoire with new techniques. That is the reason why the fans of Muay Thai claim that you never finish learning the martial art but that learning and further development are a lifelong process. If you come to know all the facets of Muay Thai, working continuously to perfect and extend your technical skills, you will become an expert in the art. Your style will fascinate your spectators during competition as well as your partners and training.

Saiyok Pumphanmuang and Khru Pit, Muay Thai Plaza Gym. Bangkok, 2000.

Table of Contents

Preface xi
Introduction xiii

Chapter 1
Background of the Competitive Sport 1

1. Development of the Competitive Sport 1
2. Stadia 10
3. Whai Khru and Ram Muay 14

Chapter 2
Competition 23

1. Competition Guidelines 23
2. Typical Mistakes 28
3. Fight Styles 30
4. Competitive Tips 32
5. Feints 36
6. Fight Preparation 41

Chapter 3
Counters against Fist Techniques 47

1. Introduction 47
2. Direct Counter 50
3. Avoid and Deflect 56
4. Block 68
5. Catch 76

Chapter 4
Counters against Elbow Techniques 79

    1. Introduction 79
    2. Direct Counter 81
    3. Avoid and Deflect 87
    4. Block 92

Chapter 5
Counters against Kicking Techniques 101

    1. Introduction 101
    2. Direct Counter 104
    3. Avoid and Deflect 112
    4. Block 115
    5. Catch 118
    6. Defense against Catch 125

Chapter 6
Counters against Pushing Foot Techniques 129

    1. Introduction 129
    2. Direct Counter 132
    3. Avoid and Deflect 134
    4. Block 142
    5. Catch 143
    6. Defense against Catch 148

Chapter 7
Counters against Knee Techniques from a Distance 151

    1. Introduction 151
    2. Direct Counter 153
    3. Avoid and Deflect 157
    4. Block 160
    5. Catch 162

Chapter 8
Counters against Clinch Techniques 165
    1. Introduction 165
    2. Control of the Opponent 168
    3. Counter against Knee Techniques 177
    4. Opening a Clinch Grip 184
    5. Counter against Grip Techniques 190

Chapter 9
Muay Thai Boran 193
    1. Introduction 193
    2. Mae Mai Muay Thai 196

Chapter 10
Training in Thailand 213
    1. Frequently Asked Questions 213
    2. Travel Arrangements 220
    3. Selecting a Gym 228

Glossary 231
Bibliography 234
The Book Team 235
Other Resources 238
Illustration Credits 242

The book team with Master Deycha, Bangkok.

Preface

I had already been involved in kickboxing for some years when I made the decision in 1995 to visit Thailand for training. I traveled to Maha Sarakham Province in northeast Thailand to learn Muay Thai. Master Deycha accepted me into his camp and invited me to live with his family. I stayed in the camp for several months and was in constant contact with my trainers, Master Deycha, Saknipon Pitakvarin, and Kempet Luksilam. This made my intensive study of Muay Thai possible. During that period I developed the concept for my first book, *Muay Thai—Kampf und Selbstverteidigung,* in 1997. The friendly relationship that I have with the people of this camp continues to this day.

From that time, my enthusiasm for Muay Thai led me to travel to Thailand for training for a few months at a time year after year. In the following years I spent many months training in Thai gyms in places like Maha Sarakham, Buriram, and Surat Thani provinces, Pattaya, and Koh Samui. In the course of these visits I had the good fortune to be trained by the legendary fighter Apideh Sit Hiran for some weeks. In all the camps I visited for training, I always received a friendly welcome and respectful treatment. The experience I had with trainers and athletes were very positive. In recent years I have lived in Thailand and was also in charge of a Muay Thai camp in the south for some time. For me, Muay Thai is an important part of my life, and it has led me to many great experiences and fascinating moments.

I believe that Muay Thai, an important component of Thai culture, should be made broadly accessible. It has brought me joy that I would like to pass on with my DVD series and books. I am grateful for the help I received in the production of my DVDs and in writing my twelve Muay Thai books so far, which have been published in German, English, Greek, Portuguese, and Spanish editions.

I hope that you can find as much satisfaction and pleasure in training and that you enjoy Muay Thai as much as I do. More information on Muay Thai is available on the internet at www.christophdelp.com, www.muaythai-book.com, www.muaythai-dvd.com, www.youtube.com/muaythaidvd, and www.facebook.com/muaythaidvd.

My sincere thanks to all those who have helped in writing this book, particularly my family, Master Deycha, Oliver Glatow, Hans-Eckhard Glatow, Taweesak Baoseehai, Ratchanu Jintanayong, Nopphadol Viwatkamolwat, Khru Khunsap, Khru Pit, Mister Pong, Apideh Sit Hiran, Menny Ossi, Amnuay Kesbumrung, Songchai Ratanasuban, Colonel Somphob Srisiri, Peraphan Rungsikulpiphat, Thomas Letté, Richard Delp, Jay, Nongnuch Rasri, and the acting athletes Khunsap, Nonsai, Saiyok, Kem, Danthai, Armin, Rit, Taweesak, Sanghai and Saraya.

Many thanks also to my trainers: Master Deycha, Apideh Sit Hiran, Khru Khunsap, Master Chalee, Raweesak, Master K, Master Wee, Master Noi, and Master Gong.

Introduction

Muay Thai, also known as Thai boxing, is a fascinating martial art that operates on a high technical level. Fighters thrill the audience with exciting performances during five rounds. They attack each other continuously and counter the opponent's attacks. To be able to hold their ground in a competition, fighters must have optimal preparation and training. Attacking techniques must be explosive, defensive and counter techniques must be carried out instinctively, and the fighter must be trained to perfection in all facets of physical fitness.

This book is the second of three in a series that describe in detail attacking techniques, defensive and counter techniques, and training. The techniques are presented by some of the best Muay Thai fighters and take into account their individual skills. I have also been able to incorporate the extensive experience of renowned Thai trainers.

This volume is dedicated in detail to defensive and counter techniques. It provides background information regarding the competitive sport. In this context, it must be kept in mind that, regardless of which attack is launched by the opponent, there are always ways to defend and ways to attack with a technique of your own. To this end, you must

About This Book

This book shows you how to develop into an advanced Thai boxer. You will get to know the best counter techniques and all the opponent's possible attacks. You will learn how to defend yourself against fist, elbow, shin, foot, and knee techniques as well as how to launch an effective counterattack. You will also find a demonstration of how to hold your ground in a clinch by controlling the opponent, how to defend against knee kicks, and how to free yourself from a grip. Test the techniques and choose a selection of them against all the opponent's attacking techniques that are best suited for your style of fighting. Perfect the techniques you have chosen by continuous training.

In this book I will also demonstrate the fifteen traditional Muay Thai techniques. Train in these techniques as well in order to develop into an advanced Thai boxer.

The section on competition provides background information, describes preparation before a fight, highlights typical mistakes, and introduces fight strategies. In addition, you will find a training schedule for preparing for a fight.

In the final chapter is all you need to know about travelling to Thailand for training. Experiencing Muay Thai where it originated will increase your performance potential by allowing you to train with the world's best Muay Thai athletes.

Let yourself be inspired by the techniques shown by some of the best Thai fighters. I wish you enjoyment and success in your training.

acquire a selection of counter techniques against all possible attacks. Learn techniques against punches, elbows, kicks, and foot and knee kicks, and perfect your conduct in a clinch. With the correct conduct in a counter technique, you will dominate your fights.

In my other books in the series, *Muay Thai Basics* (2005) and *Muay Thai Training* (2013), you will find extensive information on attacking techniques and training.

Facts Worth Knowing about Counter Techniques

Counter techniques are always both defensive and attacking techniques. The opponent's attack can either be stopped by a faster technique or be promptly countered after the initial defense. That way the opponent will be struck effectively and will be unable to continue with further techniques.

Counter techniques are classified as active or passive moves. In an active move, you foil the success of the opponent's technique with a faster technique of your own. This course of action is known as a direct counter. In a passive counter, you initially defend before promptly following up with your attacking technique. Passive counters are divided into dodging, deflecting, blocking, and catching.

This book will teach you a selection of effective counter techniques against all possible attacks by your opponent in a competition. The techniques that have been selected are frequently used by professional Thai fighters.

Trainers invariably know additional techniques, as they have had positive experiences with their application. These are not necessarily practicable for all athletes, however, as their success may be explained by individual characteristics, such as a very tall and slim body or an extraordinary reaction time. All athletes have different physical preconditions and skills, which is why some techniques are more suitable and others less suitable for you. You will quickly recognize the effectiveness that a technique has for you by repeating it in training.

Generally speaking, counter techniques have a greater chance of success the fewer steps of implementation their application has. Some trainers teach techniques that require many steps. In theory the use of such techniques is possible, but in a real fight, they are used rarely. After all, a fighter will not patiently wait for the oppenent to complete a counter technique, but rather will try to interrupt it as quickly as possible.

Put the possible counters shown here to the test. Choose techniques suitable for defense against all possible attacks. Select techniques that are best suited for your fighting style, and perfect those choices. To become a successful athlete, it is not necessary to master all the counters shown in this book. However, the more techniques you can carry out by instinct, the more difficult it will be for an opponent to figure you out.

Study the opponent's conduct in a fight. If you discover deficiencies, wait for the opportunity to exploit them. Don't always use the same techniques, but fight with varying approaches. Use the techniques shown here and grow into a versatile fighter. The counters in this book can be seen in action in my DVDs *Muay Thai—Counter against Fist and Leg Techniques* (2012) and *Muay Thai—Counter against Elbow, Knee and Clinch Techniques* (2012). You can also see many of these counters on the internet at www.youtube.com/muaythaidvd.

Advanced Counter Techniques

These days, athletes in Thai arenas excel specifically due to their powerful performances in fights. Basic techniques are used, and fights are decided with a powerful style. There are, however, many spectacular Muay Thai techniques that have the potential to prematurely end a fight. The fighting style that uses these techniques is called Muay Thai Kheaw or Muay Thai Crope Crueng, loosely translating to "Muay Thai wrestler-technique style." The use of these techniques is not easy, however, and only a few Thai teachers have mastered the style. Some of these techniques have been added to the counter techniques and are described as techniques for advanced athletes. Master Deycha teaches these techniques. More information is available from my gym at www.christophdelp.com.

Techniques in Mae Mai Muay Thai

In this book you will also find a description of the fifteen traditional Mae Mai techniques from Muay Thai Boran. These historic techniques help athletes to develop their fight conduct and make it possible to defend and counter at the same time. Advanced fighters in Muay Thai

Introduction

like to use these techniques in their competitions as they are very effective and frequently lead to an early end of the fight.

Initially, you should learn the basic techniques in depth before you train in many counter techniques. Once you have mastered the counter techniques, you can add Mae Mai techniques to your training, as their application is difficult and requires skills in basic and counter techniques. To be a good fighter, you do not have to master all the techniques shown here. Many current Thai champions are unable to use a large number of them. It is good enough to learn and use techniques that are easy to understand and and which correspond to your own talents.

Bear in mind that a large number of additional Muay Thai Boran techniques exist that can only be learned from a few teachers in Thailand. Their training should only start after extensive experience in Muay Thai.

Training Program

Once you have obtained reasonable confidence and skill in the basic techniques of attack and defense—an exact description is included in

my 2005 book *Muay Thai Basics*—you can start to study an initial selection of counter techniques. You should always try to counter after a defense; otherwise, the opponent is able to continue the attack with new techniques and without interruption.

Initially, choose three to five techniques and train for several weeks until you master them. After some weeks of training, start practicing the next counter. If you have already mastered many counters, you can also add traditional Boran techniques to your training repertoire. That way you extend your technique repertoire step by step and develop into a versatile fighter who is hard for your opponents to figure out.

You must continue to train repeatedly in the techniques you learned in order to perfect the timing of their application. You will then be able to perform the techniques ever more rapidly, more powerfully, and with better timing until you finally succeed in using them instinctively in a fight. On the other hand, it does not make any sense to train in a large number of counter techniques for only a short period. If you don't perfect the techniques, you won't be able to use them successfully in a fight. If you have to think about using a technique in a fight, the appropriate timing to apply it is already past.

Professional athletes also train in counter techniques in each training session to improve their skills. Once you know who your opponent is in the next match, your coach will train with you in specific counters tailored to the opponent's fighting characteristics.

Due to individual preconditions, it can happen that an athlete does not succeed in the application of a counter in a match despite regular training. An athlete whose footwork, for example, is slow will rarely be able to use the F6 Step Back technique against a straight punch. Under these circumstances, choose a different counter that can be used against the same attack techniques.

Introduction   xix

Important

Train in a number of counter techniques in each training session. Agree on the attack and counter technique with your training partner to attack you for some minutes with the same technique so that you can practice defending with the same technique. Then change roles and attack your partner.

Do not carry out the techniques with full power, as this can injure your partner. You must carry out the techniques precisely, however; otherwise they often may not be successful. For example, the F22 Counter Punch technique will only succeed if you stretch your body toward your opponent.

Most counters can be used against attacks from the left and right. If a specific side or the front or back of the body is important, it is pointed out. If your opponent acts in a stance that differs from your stance, apply the counter from the other side of the body.

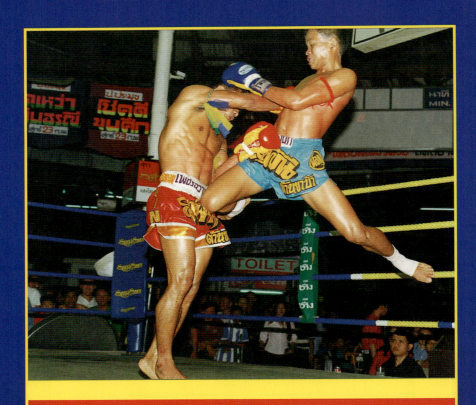

Lukporkoon Por Yodsanan carries out a jumping knee kick.
The winner was Petchawang Aborigine, Lumpinee Stadium, Bangkok, 2001.

Chapter 1
Background of the Competitive Sport

1. Development of the Competitive Sport

Muay Thai has been a competitive sport for centuries. Fights were staged at village fairs and in the course of military training. The area for the competition was marked, and the fighters competed with bandaged hands. The twentieth century saw large-scale changes, such as the construction of arenas and the use of boxing gloves. The martial art grew in popularity and gained international recognition. In recent decades Muay Thai schools have opened around the globe, and the number of people training in the sport is increasing continuously. These days there is a discussion as to what modifications are required to interest even more people in the sport so that Muay Thai gains the acceptance it deserves as part of Thai cultural heritage. It is also the aim of many enthusiasts to have Muay Thai included in the Olympics.

Acceptance and International Expansion

Muay Thai enjoys ever increasing popularity around the globe as a competitive sport and as a means of self-defense. The efficiency of the martial art has been known since the 1970s and 1980s, when athletes from other martial arts challenged Muay Thai athletes from Thailand and usually lost at an early stage. Due to interest in this effective fighting style, Muay Thai gyms opened in Europe, the Americas, and other parts of Asia. Only a few qualified trainers were available outside Thailand, however. In addition, competitions were frequently staged without approval from Muay Thai authorities in Thailand, and athletes with very differing performance levels competed. This resulted in negative media reaction to Thai boxing. The sport was described as brutal, unregulated, and low-class.

In recent years positive developments have been generated by an information campaign by the government of Thailand as well as the activities of Muay Thai enthusiasts. Numerous high-quality films about Muay Thai also led to its social acceptance and appreciation. These days a large number of Thai boxing courses are on offer, and new gyms are being opened, often with Thai trainers. The result is that the performance level outside Thailand is significantly increasing. Muay Thai fights can no longer be compared with the fights staged some years ago, which didn't contribute to a positive image of Muay Thai in terms of organization or quality.

The representatives and promoters of Muay Thai must work together more efficiently and present a common picture of Muay Thai. They must also cooperate more closely with other officials in martial art and fitness fields. Furthermore, rules and regulations have to be agreed on, and comprehensive trainer education must be introduced. If all of this comes to fruition, Muay Thai can become better established on an international scale and may even become an Olympic sport like other martial arts.

Interest in Muay Thai in Thailand

The athletic performance in Muay Thai competitions has changed over the years, influenced by the interest of spectators. Fights from the 1950s to the 1970s were described as important social events. Older Muay Thai enthusiasts describe a folk-festival atmosphere at the competitions. Families from all levels of society would go to the fights as they were admired as a form of art. To the delight of the audience, the athletes tried to impress them by using a large number of techniques. The best fighters were cultural heroes and are still frequently better known than current champions. Even back then some attendees placed bets on fight outcomes, but this was not the main reason they came to the events.

In the following decades, interests started to change, in that the Muay Thai fights in stadia and on television were mainly watched by the public with a primary interest in betting. For these spectators it was important that their favorite fighter won rather than demonstrating a large number of spectacular techniques. The volume of betting had an effect on the prize money, which prompted the athletes not to show their technical skills but instead to fight with power and energy.

Many older boxers, such as Apideh Sit Hiran, do not approve of this style, which resulted in many clinch situations. At the time, Apideh Thai boxers fought thoughtfully and attempted to achieve an early end to fights when the opportunity arose. Many of those interested in the sport were critical that in the first and second round, the athletes only tried to get a feel for each other. Many of the spectators not primarily interested in betting got bored, causing spectators and sponsors to lose interest and the prize money to go down.

Many fans of Muay Thai demanded that the art of fighting should again enjoy priority and that spectators should be entertained. The thinking was that from round one to round five, fighters should use the greatest possible number of techniques, again attracting bigger audiences that were interested in the sport and not in betting. There were many ideas from promoters, gym owners, and fans on how this could be achieved. There was a demand, for example, that the referees change their scoring.

In the end it has been movies such as *Ong-Bak: Muay Thai Warrior* and television concepts such as the *The Contender* that generated broad international interest and the willingness to provide capital. Thai investors also started to develop more interest and organized bigger events with high technical demands and purses that interested the athletes. Muay Thai also returned as a component of various programs on Thai television, and several other movies were produced after the success of *Ong-Bak*. The currently established concept of the program *Thai Fight,* in which foreign athletes compete against Thai fighters, enjoys great popularity and is also watched on television by many Thais who had no previous connection to Muay Thai. Stars in *Thai Fight* such as Kem, Buakaw, and Saiyok are once again the idols of Thai children. These fighters try to enthuse their audiences, and starting from the first round, they operate with a spectacular fighting style. Saiyok, for example, shows explosive sequences of combinations, and Kem can be observed in his desire to achieve an elbow knockout. Top Thai fighters in the weight class above 148 pounds are often booked as highlights at overseas events. Foreign spectators want to be entertained, and and they expect spectacular fighters. To generate an interested audience, Thai fighters concentrate more on Muay Thai Boran and other spectacular techniques; these fighters include Armin, for example, whose jump techniques thrill audiences and also result in knockouts.

In the lower weight categories, betting still dominates with the audiences in Thai arenas, which means that interest in the martial art and the prize money continues to be fairly low. Perhaps a stronger interest will develop in the coming years. I'm also interested to see the many television concepts with Muay Thai content that are currently in the planning stages.

Technical Development of the Fighters

When studying the fight videos of legendary top athletes like Apideh Sit Hiran, it can be seen in all the fights that all the possible basic techniques and many spectacular techniques are used with almost no interruption. Apideh, for example, continued to kick from all possible positions. A prompt spinning elbow follows a brief hold in a clinch. The fights of past legendary athletes were so fascinating and exciting that they captivated audiences and made the athletes children's heroes. In the training of former times, great importance was placed on practicing many techniques to perfection. If you have the opportunity to practice with older trainers and athletes, you will see how comprehensive their knowledge is and how realistic their demonstrations still are.

Samart Thipthamai, fighting name Samart Payakaroon, was born in 1966, and his home is Chachoengsao Province. He has fought about 175 professional fights and is a five-time Muay Thai champion and World Boxing Council (WBC) boxing champion.

Decades later, you can still observe extraordinary fighters. Dieselnoi Chor Thanasukarn mastered the knee techniques to such perfection that, by the end of his career, no one wanted to fight him any more, as a knock out was considered the inevitable conclusion. Samart Payakaroon was a good boxer with an excellent eye for the fighting situation. Somlruck Khamsing developed an extremely good eye and timing due to his intensive boxing training. In this way, he was able to thrill audiences in his later fights with the use of a variety of spectacular techniques, also originating from Muay Thai Boran. Terdkiat Sitteppitak also satisfied spectators with his tactics, understanding of the fight, and fascinating techniques. At the King Hassan Cup in Morocco, for example, he once leaned on the ropes and carried out a jumping round kick from there.

In recent decades Thai fighters have usually satisfied audiences with perfectly trained bodies, excellent timing, and powerful basic techniques. Fights were mainly decided by bodily power rather than a variety of techniques as in the past. The first rounds were characterized by cautious action in order to warm up the atmosphere for gambling instead of starting up with full power. Because of that development, fights were no longer as spectacular to watch, which resulted in shrinking audiences. Most Thai children, for example, did not know any champions unless they had a direct connection with Muay Thai.

These days, Thais have a more pronounced interest in Muay Thai and in spectacular Muay Thai performances. The higher weight classes in particular enjoy more popularity. This is taken into consideration in the training of Thai fighters, and athletes are again being trained in Boran and jump techniques.

Regarding foreign Muay Thai boxers, it is notable that their numbers are increasing. Many athletes from other countries train and fight in Thailand. In contrast to the situation twenty years ago, when only a small number of athletes visited Thailand for training, Muay Thai gyms are now filled with foreign athletes. As a consequence, the performance level of foreign athletes has significantly improved, and there are now many foreign athletes who are able to compete with the best Thai fighters.

Muay Thai offers the opportunity to captivate large numbers of people on a global scale. At this point in time, interest in Muay Thai is clearly increasing worldwide, but it is still comparatively low. Fighters must be trained to become masters in all techniques, even though training takes years. Taweesak, who is depicted in this book, inspires practitioners in his seminars abroad with his jumping and Boran techniques. To acquire his skills, he had to train with Master Deycha for a number of years. The contestants in big events, particularly those broadcast on television, must be trained to technical and athletic perfection, and if they have also acquired some spectacular techniques, they will thrill audiences. In this way, Muay Thai will find many supporters at all levels of society around the world, and television broadcasts will generate interest similar to that for traditional boxing.

Fights in the Big Arenas

In former times, only a very few top foreign fighters were permitted to participate in competitions in the two popular Muay Thai stadia, Lumpinee and Rajadamnern, both in Bangkok. These included, among others, Dany Bille, Ramon Dekker, Ivan Hippolyte, Dave Qualheim, and Rob Kaman. These days, more and more athletes are permitted to compete in these arenas, frequently including even athletes without any national titles in their home countries. This is due to the promoters' desire to satisfy the wishes of their spectators. Foreign spectators are the main source of income, with ticket prices of more than fifty U.S. dollars for one fight night at Lumpinee Stadium or Rajadamnern Stadium. Foreign visitors want to see tall athletes and foreign fighters in competition with Thai competitors, so the promoters include more foreign fighters in the program to face Thai opponents. In order to insure even matches, however, the Thai athletes are frequently not the best in Thailand. Thai spectators in the stadium rarely bet on these fights, which do not always create an exhilarating atmosphere.

The development that Thais visit the two stadia predominantly for gambling is seen as dangerous by many lovers of the sport. There is a fear that the permanent operation of Lumpinee Stadium and Rajadamnern Stadium is no longer assured without foreign spectators. In this context it must also be considered that foreign spectators are critical of the high ticket prices, and that in the first two rounds, Muay Thai athletes are just working to figure each other out. It is also apparent that some of these fights are not of a high standard. In return for high ticket prices, spectators expect fascinating fights with top athletes; otherwise they will only visit the stadium once.

The referee positions himself protectively in front of the falling Anthachai Por Sumnunchai. The winner was Lumnamoon Sor Sumalee, the Lumpinee Champion and WMC Champion, Thailand, 2000.

Other arenas in Bangkok have tried to establish themselves, including the Omnoi Stadium, which has become quite attractive to foreign visitors. The stadium frequently stages good fights in the weight categories above 148 pounds. The Omnoi's owners have also started to rethink the situation, and the events offered as a whole are now on a higher performance level. Baan Muay Thai Stadium was a nice venue with an interesting concept, but unfortunately it had to shut down due to the 2011 flood disaster. Generally speaking, there is currently a significant need to improve the presentation of Muay Thai for the international market. Great concepts such as *Thai Fight* provide a road map to how to present these events, and they will encourage stadium owners to consider new ideas.

Amateur Sport in Thailand

Muay Thai gyms in Thailand are nearly exclusively for professional athletes. Managers and trainers receive a share of the purse, which is why they try to prepare their fighters for competitions as quickly as possible. They provide their gyms with a bare minimum of equipment and accept only a limited number of athletes for training. When selecting these athletes, they look for a poor family background and that they are motivated to achieve a better lifestyle for themselves and their families. The fighters must be prepared to lead a disciplined life as a precondition for success in Muay Thai. Gyms are frequently visited by gamblers who exert much influence in Muay Thai due to the high stakes.

Affluent parents do not want their children to train in such places. They are, however, aware of the many positive effects of martial arts training on the physical development of their children, which is why they want them trained in other martial arts. Against this background, tae kwon do gyms have opened up around Thailand with training exclusively for amateurs. That situation prompted the Thai government to promote Muay Thai, part of the cultural heritage of Thailand. There are currently attempts to establish Muay Thai as an amateur sport on a large scale, and many control mechanisms are being employed in the professional version. This has resulted in a greater acceptance of Muay Thai at all levels of society.

A number of gyms have been established that are financed by income generated by training amateurs. They are properly equipped and strictly controlled. Anyone can train in these gyms regardless of age, gender, or athletic background. Different courses that vary by performance level are offered, and students receive a certificate at the end. This is also true at fitness studios in Bangkok and other large towns, where a great interest in Muay Thai exists and where courses have traditionally only been offered for competitive athletes.

> ### Interview with Niyom Lagsanapang
>
> Under his fighting names Niyom Sit Hiran and Niyom Ratanasit, Niyom Lagsanapang appeared in more than three hundred professional fights. He has been the Thai champion several times and thus the best international fighter in his division. In addition, he was listed among the best Thai fighters for approximately six years. Specific mention must be made of his fight as Rajadamnern champion versus the Lumpinee champion at the time, Rerngchai Srisothorn, which he won by knockout in the first round.
>
> This interview is from 2000, when we met in his hometown, Surat Thani.
>
> **Christoph Delp:** Where does your interest in Muay Thai come from, and at what age did you start training?
>
> **Niyom Lagsanapang:** The sport was very popular at the time, and I was also fascinated with it. If I didn't have the money to pay for a ticket, I would climb a nearby tree and watch the fights from there. At the age of twelve, I started with regular training.
>
> **Christoph:** When did you have your first fight?
>
> **Niyom:** I had my first fight at the age of ten, without any previous training. A fighter was needed at a festival, and I volunteered. I won this particular children's competition and had a nice ring experience, which led me to start with regular training.
>
> **Christoph:** How many fights did you have, and what was your rate of success?
>
> **Niyom:** I had more than three hundred professional fights and was a two-time champion. In 1954 I defeated Rerngchai Srisothorn, the Lumpinee Champion at the time, by knockout in the first round.
>
> **Christoph:** At what age did you finish your career, and what did you do afterward?

Niyom: I had my last fight at age thirty-three. Subsequently I worked for some time as a manager and trainer. I didn't have the success I had hoped for, however, so that I retired from the profession after a number of years. After that I opened my own specialty fish shop. Today I'm a pensioner.

Christoph: Are you still active in sports?

Niyom: After my active time as fighter, I trained in various types of sport. I'm still jogging and regularly ride my bicycle.

Christoph: Do you still watch Muay Thai fights, and have there been changes from the time you were active?

Niyom: I regularly watch fights, and I can see many changes. Today's fights are dominated by power instead of using the brain, so fights come to many clinch situations. This is neither attractive to watch nor particularly efficient. Today's purses are much higher than in the past, although we used to have a far bigger audience. There was some betting then, but not as much.

Christoph: What do you think of the athletic development of foreigners who enter fights in Thailand?

Niyom: The foreigners are improving. Frequently I like their style. They apply many different techniques and are particularly well trained in boxing techniques. There are only a few good foreign boxers in the lower weight classes. However, the higher the weight class, the more the situation changes in their favor.

Christoph: Did you ever sustain a serious injury during a fight? And what is your physical condition now?

Niyom: I have never incurred a serious injury, and I am in good shape even today.

2. Stadia

Thailand has two big arenas: Lumpinee Stadium and Rajadamnern Stadium, both in Bangkok, and both home to several fights each week. The atmosphere at these events is extraordinary. Thousands of spectators yell and shout to encourage their favorite athletes. Many tourists recall a visit to such an event as an unforgettable experience.

Muay Thai Champions promoting a Songchai Ratanasuban event, July 2001.
Left to right: first person unknown, Pornsane Sitmonchai, Sayannoi Royalrainbow, Thaweesak Singklongsri, Ngatoo Antharungroj, Anuwat Kaewsamrit, Thongchai Tor Silachai, Pet-Ake Detchoosri, and Boevy Sor Udomsorn.

Lumpinee Stadium

Lumpinee Stadium is internationally renowned for its Muay Thai and boxing events. Since December 8, 1956, it has been a venue for regular fights. Before Lumpinee Stadium's completion, Rajadamnern Stadium was the only venue in Bangkok, so athletes had long waits between fights. Lumpinee Stadium was established to protect Muay Thai and to enable athletes to compete in more fights.

The stadium was also meant improve the chances of success for classical boxers in international competition, for example at the Olympic

Background of the Competitive Sport

The longtime mini flyweight champion Yodsaenglai Petyindee, left, and the longtime super featherweight champion Samkor Chor Ratchatasupak.

Lumpinee Champions as of February 2012

Mini flyweight (not over 105 pounds): vacant; number-one challenger: Nikomlek Tor Tawat
Light flyweight (not over 108 pounds): vacant; number-one challenger: Superlek Kiatmoo 9
Flyweight (not over 112 pounds): vacant; number-one challenger: Phetchartchay Chaoraiooy
Super flyweight (not over 115 pounds): Wanchalong Sitzornong
Bantamweight (not over 118 pounds): Kaotam Lookphrabath
Super bantamweight (not over 122 pounds): Sam A. Tor Rattanakiat
Featherweight (not over 126 pounds): Paneak Sitnumnoi
Super featherweight (not over 130 pounds): F-16 Rajannot
Lightweight (not over 135 pounds): Saketdow Phatpayathai
Super lightweight (not over 140 pounds): Damial Kwaytonggym
Welterweight (not over 147 pounds): Aikpracha Meenayotin
Super welterweight (not over 154 pounds): Saiyok Pumphanmuang

Games, thereby bringing honor to Thailand. The stadium is controlled by the Thai army and is also used for army events. The first manager was Lieutenant Colonel Erb Saengrit, who was in charge of Lumpinee Stadium until June 1961. He rapidly established its national reputation for Muay Thai fights and international boxing events.

Address

Lumpinee Boxing Stadium
Rama 4 Road, Patumwan, Bangkok
muaythailumpinee@yahoo.com
www.muaythailumpini.com
Operating hours: early evening Tuesday, Friday, and Saturday
Ticket prices vary depending on the distance from the ring and cost 2,000–3,000 baht.

Rajadamnern Stadium

Next to Lumpinee Stadium, Rajadamnern Stadium is the best-known arena for Thai boxing competitions.

History

In 1941 the tenth prime minister of Thailand, Field Marshal P Pibulsongkram, gave orders for a national boxing stadium to be built. A plot on Rajadamnern Nok Road was chosen for the project, and it is still there today. Construction started on March 1, 1941, but work was suspended temporarily due to supply shortages during World War II. In 1945 work restarted, and the project was finished in four months; the first fights took place on December 23, 1945. For the first four years, the stadium had no roof. In 1949, a roof was planned, and modernization continued through 1951, which also saw the capacity of the stadium increased.

The stadium was managed by the government for its first seven years but operated at a loss, which is why it was then leased to a Thai firm. The manager at the time, Chalerm Cheosakul, requested permission to continue his work and founded the Rajadamnern Co. Ltd. on May 24, 1953, and the firm has operated the stadium since then. Over time the stadium has become one of the best-known international arenas for Muay Thai and is considered a Thai institution.

Address

Rajadamnern Stadium
Rajadamnern Nok Road, Pompab Satroo Pai, 10200 Bangkok
info@rajadamnern.com
www.rajadamnern.com
Operating hours: early evening Sunday, Monday, and Wednesday. Ticket prices vary depending on the distance from the ring and cost 2,000–3,000 baht.

Rajadamnern Champions as of February 2012

Mini flyweight (not over 105 pounds): Phet Lookmakarmwan
Light flyweight (not over 108 pounds): Dedkart Por Pongsawang
Flyweight (not over 112 pounds): Lamnammoon Sakchaichote
Super flyweight (not over 115 pounds): Farsawang Thor Siangtiannoi
Bantamweight (not over 118 pounds): Kompichit Sor Kor Siripong
Super bantamweight (not over 122 pounds): Kaimookdam Aikbangzai
Featherweight (not over 126 pounds): Sirimongkon P. K. Muaythai
Super featherweight (not over 130 pounds): Jomtong Chuwattana
Lightweight (not over 135 pounds): Nopakrit Kor Kumpanart
Super lightweight (not over 140 pounds): Hiroki Ishi
Welterweight (not over 147 pounds): Numpon P. K. Sterio
Super welterweight (not over 154 pounds): Kanongsuek Chuwattana
Middle weight (not over 160 pounds): Lamsongcram Chuwattana

Promoters

All arenas have promoters responsible for organizing the fights. It is their job to satisfy the audiences and to enable interesting and high-caliber competitions. Small village festivals also have events that must be planned and organized by a promoter. Songchai Ratanasuban, the most prominent promoter in Thailand, also first gained experience organizing Muay Thai competitions in villages.

Songchai Ratanasuban became popular as a promoter in Lumpinee Stadium by providing the best fighters and interesting matches in his program. He also made it possible to watch the events on television. At a later stage he was also active as a promoter at Rajadamnern Stadium. In accordance with his slogan, "Muay Thai—Thai heritage—world heritage," he promotes Muay Thai on a global scale. He organizes, for

Songchai Ratanasuban, Somlruck Khamsing, and Christoph, Bangkok, 2002.

example, events in France, the Netherlands, the United States, Morocco, and Japan.

3. Whai Khru and Ram Muay

Whai Khru and Ram Muay are dance ceremonies performed by the athletes prior to Muay Thai competitions. It is often mistakenly assumed that these

Interview with Songchai Ratanasuban

Songchai Ratanasuban was interviewed by the author at Rajadamnern Stadium in July 2001.

Christoph Delp: What does Muay Thai mean to you?

Songchai Ratanasuban: Muay Thai is part of Thai heritage. Nobody knows exactly at what point in the past this type of martial art was created. Documentation exists dating back more than four hundred years. I believe, however, that the martial art has existed since Thailand came into being. In the past it was employed for protection against one's enemies.

Muay Thai started to spread internationally approximately twenty years ago. In comparison to all types of martial arts, Muay Thai is the most effective. It can be used to promote international awareness and the popularity of Thailand.

Christoph: How long you have been interested in Muay Thai?

Songchai: I liked Muay Thai even as a small child. At the age of sixteen I started to train and had a few fights at events at village festivals. At the age of nineteen I began to be active as a promoter of Muay Thai competitions, and I was successful. At age twenty-four I moved to Bangkok as a promotion assistant for Lumpinee Stadium and Rajadamnern Stadium. I continue to work as a promoter to this day.

Christoph: What are the differences between today's fighting styles compared to those of the past?

are Buddhist ceremonies. Thai people take much pride in their traditional performances, which have been handed down for centuries. To be courteous, foreign fighters should also perform the Whai Khru and Ram Muay. In accordance with the sequence prior to the fight, the paragraphs below describe the initial access to the ring, then the Whai Khru, followed by the Ram Muay. This is the usual procedure, but it may vary slightly.

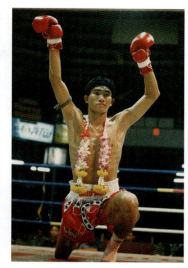

Somlruck Khamsing, fighting name Peemanamlek Sitaran, performs the Whai Khru. Born in 1973, Somiruck lives in Kon Kaen Province, and his training camp is Jocky Gym. He has been in approximately 250 professional fights, and he was a 1996 Olympic boxing champion.

Songchai: In the past all types of techniques were used in fights. The fighters were heavier than today because not so much attention was paid to their weight. These days the competitions are more balanced because the technical level and the fitness of the fighters are of a similar standard.

Christoph: How has the quality of foreign fighters changed?

Songchai: Approximately twenty-five years ago, Thom Hanrick, from the Netherlands, came with his students from the Chakuriki Gym to Thailand [in 1978]. Without exception, these athletes lost all their fights. Currently, he is a famous promoter in Europe, and his athletes compete at a high level. The foreign athletes are taller and therefore dominate Thai athletes in the heavier weight divisions. Thai fighters continue their dominance in the lighter weight divisions.

Christoph: What are your future plans in Muay Thai?

Songchai: So far I have organized fights in France, the Netherlands, Australia, Morocco, and Japan. It's my aim to establish and promote Muay Thai in more countries.

Christoph: Is there anything else you would like to tell the readers of this book?

Songchai: Read this book on the art of Muay Thai carefully. Muay Thai is the best way to fight. It is also suitable for self-defense, and regular training will lead to overall physical fitness.

Prior to the Start of Whai Khru

On their way to the ring, Thai boxers may kneel in front of the ring steps and perform a *wai,* a traditional Thai greeting. Their hands are held at chin level with the fingers pointing upward. In this way, the fighters express their respect for the venue where the fight is held. No one is obliged to kneel at this point, however. In addition, before they set foot on the steps to the ring, fighters can exhale through the nostrils. The first step is then accessed with the foot on the same side that was easier to breathe through.

Prior to entering the ring, a wai must always be performed in front of the rope. This shows respect for the ring and the performances in it. Some Thai boxers also believe that there is a ring spirit that they can appease with a wai. Subsequently, the attendants pull the rope down, and the Thai boxers jump across. Some of the fighters run their hands along the rope before they actually move across.

In the center of the ring, a wai is performed outward in all four directions to the audience, and the fighter bows. This is one way of thanking the spectators for coming to see the fight. From the center of the ring, the fighters return to their corners, where they perform a wai. The ceremony of entering the ring is then complete, and the fighters sit on their chairs and wait until the music for the Whai Khru starts.

Description of Whai Khru

Once the orchestra begins to play, the fighters take three steps to the center of the ring, stand still in an upright position, and take a deep breath to calm down.

Tep Pa Nom

Kneel down, put your left instep on the floor, and then put your right instep on the sole of your left foot. The upper part of your body is kept upright, and the palms of your hands are held together at chest level, with the fingers pointing upward (photo A).

Wirun Fongnoon (Roon), fighting name Arun Sor Fongnom, was born in 1984 and has had many professional fights; she is a former world champion.

Bending to the Floor

Next, bend the upper part of your body to the front, and initially place your left hand, then your right hand, on the floor. Then the upper part of your body returns to its original position; your right hand is lifted first. The entire procedure is repeated twice. During the last exercise, remain in the lower position for about twenty seconds and meditate. This meditation is meant to show respect for important people and to request their help for a win (photo B).

Ta Wai Bang Com

Return to the opening position of Tep Pa Nom, raise your toes, and spread your knees. In the process, remain seated on your heels. Your arms then start to move to the rhythm of the music as follows: First, move your arms backward down, turning your hands so that the backs of your hands are ultimately pointing down. Concurrently, the upper part of your body stretches forward. Your hands then return in a large circular motion to your chest, so that at the end of the movements, your hands are next to each other and your thumbs are resting on your chest. At the same time, the upper part of your body is raised again. Finally, your arms are stretched out and raised, your head slightly retracts, and your thumbs move to your forehead (photo C). The entire exercise is repeated twice.

Ta Patom

One foot is now moved to the front to support the weight of your body, and the upper part of your body bends forward. In the process, your wrists circle around each other (photo D).

Prom

Next, your rear foot is lifted, and your wrists circle around each other three times. Your rear foot then rests again on your toes, and your weight is shifted to that foot. Your front leg is slightly stretched.

Tep Ni Mit

For the last move, get up with your rear foot (photo E) while your wrists circle around each other. Your front foot returns to the floor, and the Whai Khru finishes with a bow (photo F).

Muay Thai Counter Techniques

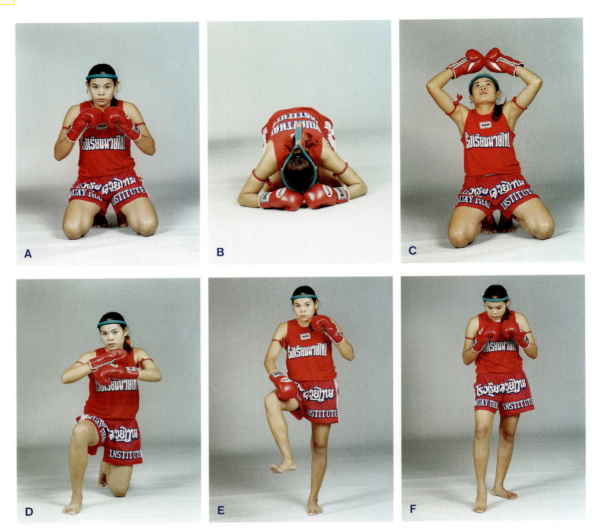

A. Tep Pa Nom, start of the position. B. Bending to the Floor. C. Ta Wai Bang Com. D. Ta Patom. E and F. Tep Ni Mit.

Ram Muay

Ram Muay combines different dance styles with one type of exercise. Through its performance, fighters honor their trainer and their gym. They concentrate on and remember their own skills and tactics and their trainer's advice. Ram Muay helps the contestants to calm their nerves and mentally prepare for the fight. The exercise is also a form of body stretching.

In earlier times, Muay Thai experts could determine a fighter's home camp from the Ram Muay, as each camp taught a specific exercise. Nowadays, many fighters have their own style, which makes it difficult to determine their camp.

Background of the Competitive Sport

Ram Muay follows immediately after the end of the Whai Khru. For its performance, a special type of walk is employed for all position changes, such as Yaang Sam Khum, which is very popular.

Yaang Sam Khum

First, lift your front foot and raise the toes (photo A). Now rest the toes on the floor in front of your body, shift your foot to the outside, and slightly turn your body. In the final position, the entire foot is resting on the floor, and the exercise is repeated with the other foot (photo B). Continue until the desired position in the ring has been reached.

A and B. Yaang Sam Khum.

Variations of Ram Muay

For Ram Muay, fighters choose a traditional style, combine styles, or create their own show. The best-known traditional styles are Pra Ram Plang Sorn, Hong Hern, Nok Yoong Fhon Hang, Nok Yoong Ram Pan, Sord Soi Ma La, Pa Yak Pom Gnang, Guang Leaw Long, Sua Lag Hang, and Saw Noi Pra Pang.

Pra Ram Plang Sorn

After the Whai Khru, the athlete moves to the site for the Ram Muay with his or her particular type of walk. The Pra Ram Plang Sorn style is usually started from the center of the ring. Take one step in the direction of your opponent, one step in the direction of the opposite corner, and then turn again with one step toward your opponent. Once the desired position has been reached, stretch your front arm and move your rear arm as if pulling an arrow and releasing it (photo A). After the move, put your front foot hard on the floor. Next, hold your leading hand in front of your face and see whether the imaginary arrow has hit its mark (photo B). Success or failure is expressed by nodding or shaking your head. There is usually an indication of two failures before success is signaled.

During the entire performance, move your body to the rhythm of the music. Proceed with your chosen type of walk to your opponent, and stamp the floor with your front foot three times. Finally, return with your walk to your corner. This concludes the Ram Muay.

These days fighters sometimes indicate weapons other than a bow and arrow. For reasons of tradition, this is not necessarily appreciated by some backers of the sport.

A and B. Drawing the imaginary bow and verifying whether the arrow has hit its target.

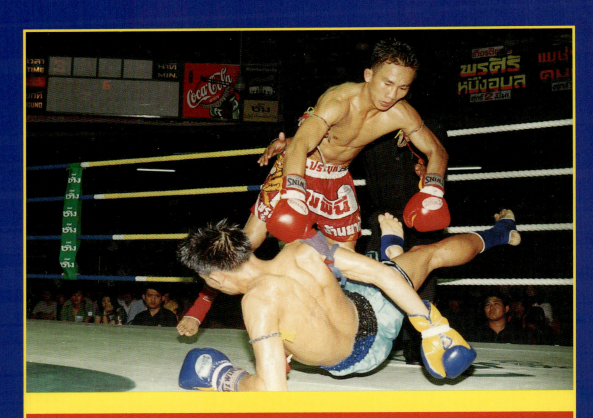

Pornsawan Por Pramook, Lumpinee champion, throws Saemsook Por Kaewsaen in a clinch. Pornsawan won. Lumpinee Stadium, 2000.

Chapter 2
Competition

1. Competition Guidelines

To succeed in a Muay Thai competition, you must observe the following rules of fight preparation and fight conduct.

Preparation

High competitive goals can only be achieved through proper preparation. You must assume that you will meet an opponent whose technical and physical performance is as high as yours, if not higher. Proper preparation can provide you with the opportunity to gain an advantage, which will be decisive for a victory.

In the course of prepping for a fight, you must eliminate all stress factors that could distract you from your training in the following weeks. Speak to your partner, family, and friends and inform them of your plans so that they are aware of and sensitive to the intensive process you'll will be going through.

Your training schedule must be challenging, and your weight must be strictly controlled. Only athletes who are hard on themselves will develop the optimum performance levels and the correct mental approach for competition. The lifestyle of a fighter must be tailored to the athletic competition; you might need more sleep than usual, and therefore, you should maintain a regular sleep schedule. Use restorative measures, such as the sauna and massages, to help speed up recovery time, thereby preventing excessive physical strain. Intensive preparation is also important for self-confidence—knowing you're performing at an optimum level will increase your self-assurance in a match.

Mongkol Karlek, fighting name Sakmongkol Sitchoochok, was born in 1973. His home is Prachinburi Province, and he has had about 144 professional fights. He is a former Lumpinee champion and WMC champion in the welterweight division.

Weighing In

If you exceed the weight limit on the day of the fight, you can still quickly lose two or three pounds by sweating. The maximum is three pounds, as shedding that much water weight before a fight will reduce your performance, and shedding any more is dangerous. Fighters frequently prefer skipping rope or jogging to induce sweating. The athlete wears warm clothing to increase body temperature and to generate more sweat. Skipping rope should be done at an even pace, not at a fast heart rate, to save energy for the fight. Subsequently, the skin is firmly rubbed with towels, which can reduce the weight a little further.

Drink plenty of fluids—water and sports drinks—after weighing in, but drink slowly. Eat easily digestible food and chew slowly. Fitness bars and bananas are recommended. Do not eat too much, avoid fatty or spicy foods, and avoid foods that you are not accustomed to, as they may cause stomach cramps. If you have sufficient time prior to the competition, you can have another easily digestible serving about one hour after the first small meal.

Conduct Prior to the Fight

Concentrate on the competition and collect your thoughts. Visualize your long and ascetic training and keep in mind that you can now demonstrate why you went through the grueling process. You must completely concentrate on the fight, and you must not be concerned about anything else. Your training staff must protect you from any external influence that could take your mind off the fight. It is therefore important to be surrounded by individuals you can trust.

Start warming up at an early stage. After the usual warm-up exercises and stretching, it is recommended to do light shadowboxing and to recall fight tactics. Also, do a warm-up on pads to gain a feeling for distance. You should avoid intensive training on the pads with powerful techniques so as not to waste any energy before the fight. You must clearly increase your heart rate a number of times, however, so that you are warmed up enough to call on your full performance from round one; that way an opponent rush toward you at the sound of the bell won't catch you by surprise. You can increase your heart rate by shadowboxing, skipping rope, and swift but not powerful work on the pads.

Fight Conduct

Enter the ring or the fight area with self-assurance. Breathe regularly and stay relaxed. Pay particular attention to your neck muscles, keeping them consciously relaxed, as some athletes get very tense prior to a competition and apply extreme tension to their neck muscles. Nervousness prior to a competition differs from athlete to athlete and improves through the athlete's career. If you enter the ring hyped up and nervous, you lose valuable energy for the fight. Visualize your strong points. Know that you are now prepared to fight. Take pride in your intensive training, and look forward to showing off your hard-won skills.

Perform some relaxed moves in the ring to get a feeling for the ring and the floor. Fall back lightly into the ropes to get a feeling for the tension. Think of your fight tactics; you must be prepared for your opponent to rush you as soon as the fight starts.

Welcome your opponent prior to the fight, and show respect for his or her athletic performance. Remember that your opponent has also endured a long and ascetic preparation. Your objective, however, is to win, so you are now allowed to do whatever you need to do to win the fight as long as it conforms to the rules. Give the impression that you are convinced of your victory. You can also intimidate your opponent by gestures, for example by staring aggressively in the eyes. Some means of provocation, however, are not acceptable, including abuse, spitting, and the conscious use of illegal techniques such as attacks to the genitals. An athlete who does this repeatedly will be disqualified.

Whai Khru and Ram Muay help develop full concentration for the fight.

Concentrate on the competition, and don't let your rhythm be disturbed by calls from the audience. You know that you will also have to take hard hits, so don't get tensed up or nervous. Always stay in control, keep your cool, and resist any temptation for rash action or overly hasty counterattacks. If you fight without control, you'll be in danger of being hit by an effective counter technique, which may cause you to lose the fight early on. Avoid being drawn into wild exchanges of punches and kicks, and always maintain control of the fight situation.

Keep moving and use the entire area of the ring. Avoid being driven into a corner: always move away to the side if you feel yourself backing into the ropes. If you remain in a fixed position, your opponent will find it easy to figure you out.

Always maintain a strong fight stance, and move with confidence; you want to show your opponent that you are still fit and able to fight. Mislead your opponent, feint, and keep him or her on the move. Never show any weakness or pain. If your opponent realizes that you have been affected by a technique and that you have a weak point, your opponent will concentrate on that part of the body. Even when you are struck by an effective blow, you must create the impression for the audience and the referees that your opponent's technique was harmless. Always create the impression of superiority. This can demoralize your opponent in a hard fight and can be the decisive edge in the final count.

After the fight, respectfully bid good-bye to your opponent. You both did your best, and this must be respected.

Breaks between Rounds

Prior to the fight it is important for you and your trainer to agree on your exact conduct during breaks. If the coach sees that you are moving slowly after the bell, he or she must promptly come toward you and walk with you to your corner. People should not get the impression that you are groggy, even though you might be.

You must rest and relax during the break, concentrate, and take deep breaths in preparation for the next round. The coach can massage your neck, which is of particular importance if you are tense and nervous.

The coach must give you clear and precise directions for the next round. Pay no attention to other people shouting irrelevant information from outside the ring. It is also of no help to you if the coach accompanies these instructions with nervous gestures. You must be able to rely on only one person to give you precise directions on your fight conduct. Such directions can relate to your mistakes, your opponent's weak points, and recommendations on counter techniques. The coach may demand that you repeat the tactics for the fight in detail so that they are better ingrained in your memory.

Between Tournament Bouts

Always keep warm by shadowboxing and stretching between matches. Prior to each match in the tournament, particularly after a lengthy break, it is important that you increase your heart rate with easy punches and kicks to the pads and by skipping rope. You must also prepare for the tactics of each fight with light shadowboxing.

Drink plenty of fluids between matches, especially water, mineral water, and sports drinks. As before, bananas and fitness bars are recommended foods. Do not eat too much, and avoid spicy foods as well as foods that you are not accustomed to, as these may lead to stomach cramps.

Postfight Recovery

After a fight, give your body a rest from training. This will help your body recover and will help you regain a clear head and accumulate new energy. The body requires some time to recover after several weeks of fight preparation, before you can start with the next training program. This procedure is important to be able to achieve progressive performance improvements and eventually maximum performance. The recovery phase must be extended in accordance with the intensity of the preparatory phase and fight effort.

You should resume gentle sporting activities, though, no later than one week after a fight. This could include, for example, light jogging at a low heart rate to insure that your physical performance does not deteriorate and your weight does not increase significantly. A complete rest of more than one week will have a negative effect on your performance level.

Peerapong Chuanpoe, fighting name Boevy Sor Udomsorn, was born in 1984. His home is Kalasin Province, and he trains at Kietshansing Camp in Bangkok. As of January 2012 he has had about 140 professional fights, and he is a former flyweight Rajadamnern champion.

2. Typical Mistakes

The tactics of a Muay Thai fighter are of vital significance in achieving high competitive goals. Whether or not a fighter succeeds in imposing a fight style on the match and thereby controlling the action is of decisive importance to the outcome of a competition.

Certain mistakes arise in competitions time and again and must definitely be avoided.

Slow Start

You must be focused and ready to deliver your techniques from the moment the bell rings. If you start the first round slowly and passively, you will frequently be unable to compensate for the lost points in the following rounds. This applies particularly to amateur Muay Thai bouts, in which matches are scheduled for only a few rounds. A loss of points from the first round can also mean that the original fight tactics must be abandoned to score points through aggressive action, or to achieve a premature end to the fight. Such an approach, however, is rarely successful and instead involves the great risk that you will move into your opponent's hard technique, which could mean the early end of the fight for you.

Hasty Start

If you rush toward your opponent in the first round and attack with wild punches, aiming to break your opponent's will and self-assurance or even to succeed in a premature end of the fight, you will waste a lot of power and energy. Success in such an exchange of blows is determined by physical preconditions and not by the tactics of Muay Thai. You don't learn anything about fight conduct and the mistakes of your opponent, which is vital for the rest of the match. For your opponent, it is usually relatively easy to defend the onrush, and once your stamina is affected on account of the intensive attack, your opponent can counter effectively. It is a general rule that fighters who start the first round with undue haste experience considerable physical difficulties in subsequent rounds.

Passive and One-Sided Fight Styles

Don't restrict your fight style to passive defense measures. If you react primarily with defensive techniques without subsequent counters, your opponent can continue to attack without interruption. You should always follow up your defensive techniques with attacking techniques of your own.

Maintain your concentration, and don't get nervous and adopt your opponent's fight style. Stay versatile and don't just use a limited number of techniques, as this makes it easy for your opponent to figure you out. Often athletes concentrate on fist techniques and use only few leg techniques. This approach leaves you unable to prepare for effective techniques and combinations; you'll have to wait until your opponent offers you the opportunity to apply a technique.

Left to right: Nonsai Sor Sanyakorn, Saiyok Pumphanmuang, and Prakaisaeng Sit Or/Kaeyanghaadao.

3. Fight Styles

The following fight styles can frequently be seen in the ring, and you must learn their defense by heart. Bear in mind that your opponent can change fight tactics in the course of the competition if these do not turn out to be successful and he or she falls behind in points.

The jumping knee kick is an extremely effective special technique that captivates the audience.

Fighters with Special Techniques

These fighters have mastered a particular offensive technique that they employ often. This can be a fist technique such as a rear straight punch, an elbow technique, a knee kick from behind, or a kicking technique such as a round kick. The application of these special attacking techniques is frequently a great danger for the opponent.

Try to stop the use of the technique. If your opponent is known for a powerful rear straight punch, for example, you can repeatedly deliver techniques to your opponent's punching arm, such as round kicks and straight knee kicks. Several kicks to the upper arm can also foil your opponent's effective use of a special technique. You must also study your opponent and find out in which fight situations he or she usually delivers the special technique. If you are successful, you can feint, causing your opponent to employ the special technique. Because you are expecting the technique, you will be able to avoid the blow and counter with an effective technique of your own.

Distance Fighters

Rather tall fighters with particularly good kicking skills frequently attempt to conduct the match from a distance. You must bridge the distance to this type of opponent to be able to deliver effective attacks from a medium or close distance. If possible, push your opponent into the corner of the ring and work with side hooks, body hooks, and elbow techniques. Use feints and quick combinations to set up the chance to move forward. If you are successful with a feint, or if you land a combination, you can then move forward. Keep your upper body in motion so that you do not offer a fixed target. If you have the opportunity for a forward move, for example after deflection of a technique to the side, you must move in a flash with your guard raised. However, if this is carried out too quickly and your opponent reads your intention, he or she will launch an effective counterattack.

Some distance fighters specialize in counter techniques. These fighters require versatile reactions. Your opponent tries to figure you out and read your techniques at an early stage and thus deliver effective counters. You must therefore work with many evasive moves and feints so that your opponent changes position and you can perform different combinations of techniques.

Close Fighters

A fighter who has developed special skills in fist and elbow techniques and who has a rather powerful build often seeks the infight in order to deliver effective techniques. Clinching experts seek the infight in order to grab and control the opponent before they deliver effective knee techniques.

You must try to keep your opponent at a distance to prevent the use of these skills. Use jabs, push kicks, and side kicks from the front leg. These techniques will keep your opponent away, interrupting the techniques, and enable you to set up your combinations. Avoid exchanging punches with these fighters. If your opponent rushes forward, don't let yourself be pushed back into a corner; step away to the side. You should also do feints, tempting your opponent to rush forward, so that you can counter with an effective technique. Straight knee kicks from a distance in combination with straight punch techniques are also an appropriate means.

Close fighters seek the infight for control of the opponent.

Swift and Tricky Fighters

These athletes move with quick steps toward and away from the opponent. They deliver quick combinations and use many feints and evasive moves. Don't be misled and attempt to adopt your opponent's fight pace; instead try to maintain your own fighting style. Take a position in the center of the ring, hold this position, and study your opponent's fight conduct. In the process, also try to maintain the best suitable distance by keeping your opponent busy. You must not follow hastily, however, but rather move and turn with your opponent in the center of the ring.

Deliver strong punches, kicks, and knee kicks to restrict your opponent's movements. If you succeed with a blow and your opponent loses some sense of coordination, you must quickly follow up with powerful punching techniques. Then try to push your opponent into the corner of the ring and continue your attacks.

Fighters in a Different Stance

In the case of a hard-hitting fighter who uses a different stance, you must make sure that you do not move to the side of your opponent's rear punching arm. You can keep your opponent away with jabs, push kicks, and knee kicks from the front. You should also repeatedly deliver combinations that include a front hook, in the process of which you move to the outside, away from the punching arm. In a conventional stance against a southpaw, move left to the outside; as a southpaw up against a fighter with a conventional stance, move right to the outside.

If your opponent uses a large number of jabs, push kicks, and knee kicks from the front, reduce the target area as much as possible. Study your opponent's fight conduct in detail and use counter techniques that stop the success of the opponent's punching and kicking techniques. Your opponent will turn more and more to techniques from the rear part of the body, which are easier to identify and defend against.

4. Competitive Tips

In a fight, you must always be unpredictable to your opponent. You must continuously feint and apply new techniques. You can disturb your opponent's timing with tricks, provoke him or her, and even achieve a knockout. A front kick to the face, for example, is considered insulting and will be cheered by the audience. As a consequence, a speedy counter can be expected after such a technique. This counter is frequently not well planned, so you can block it and carry out an effective hit.

Competitive tips I have acquired in the course of my travels to Thailand are briefly listed in the following sections. These tricks should be included in your training as a matter of course. Only then can they be applied successfully in competition.

In this context, I would like to extend special thanks to Apideh Sit Hiran, one of the best boxers of all time, who has taken much time to transfer his knowledge to me.

Christoph (left) and Apideh Sit Hiran during training, Fairtex Gym, Bangkok, 2000. Apideh was born in 1935 and has had approximately three hundred professional fights. He is a seven-time champion as well as a challenger in boxing for the WBA and WBC title. Apideh is considered a living Muay Thai legend, and to many people, he is the best fighter of all time. He has also been very successful as a trainer at Fairtex Gym in Bangkok and has worked in the United States.

Feint and Front Kick

Start with a round kick to the leg, change the direction of the kick movement to the top, and apply a front kick. With the ball of your foot, make contact with your opponent's nose, throat, or eye area. For a hard hit or even a knockout, use the rear of your foot. A kick with your front foot is meant to provoke your opponent. Apideh frequently applied this technique in his fights.

As an alternative, start with a front kick to the body by raising your leg slightly. The leg is then quickly returned to the floor. If you succeed in misleading your opponent into dropping cover to some extent, you should carry out a straight punch as you lower your leg. If you feinted the front kick with your right leg, you should also punch from that side. If you feinted with your left, punch from the left.

Feint and Round Kick

For this trick, repeatedly feint the start of a round kick, to which end your hip is slightly turned in and back. This irritates your opponent and will cause him or her to lose time for a defense. Subsequently, you actually follow up with the round kick.

A. The kick against the pivot leg.

This trick can be carried out with your front or rear foot. To use your front foot, you must transfer your weight to your rear leg. This technique can induce your opponent to use one of his or her own weapons, which you, however, should anticipate and be able to counter effectively. Apideh also demonstrated this technique to perfection in his matches.

Front Kick to the Pivot Leg

This technique is aimed at your opponent's pivot leg (see photo A). Use this technique parallel to your opponent's round kick, when your opponent is unable to defend. Apideh applies this kick with his heel and a lateral position of his foot for a firmer stance. In training sessions, the ball of your foot should be used, as the heel is very hard.

Particularly suitable targets are the inner side of your opponent's thigh and the knee. A hard execution of the technique can result in a knockout.

Return Strike with the Elbow

This technique is used after a rotating elbow or side elbow has missed the head. Supported by a move of the hip, you promptly return your elbow in a direct line and hit your opponent's chin.

If your elbow fails to make contact, your opponent will usually attack, opening up an opportunity for full contact with your return strike. Should your opponent not attack, you must take a step toward your opponent for better impact of the blow.

Defense against a Knee Kick

This technique should be employed in clinch situations with great care. If the blow has no particular impact on your opponent, he or she is able to counter with a side elbow technique.

If your opponent uses a straight knee from a distance, you can strike the thigh with the tip of your elbow. Next, use this elbow for a rotating elbow or an uppercut elbow. You can also carry out a spinning elbow.

Strike with the Shoulder in Clinch Situations

In clinch situations, this technique is used to hit your opponent's chin with your shoulder. To this end, slightly turn toward your opponent, bend your front leg, and strike upward. In the process, your weight is shifted toward your opponent. The power for this technique is generated by lowering and stretching your leg, shifting your weight, and the shoulder move. Apideh explained that this technique can lead to the premature conclusion of a fight.

Kick with the Heel in Clinch Situations

This technique is useful in a clinch situation. Kick your opponent's thigh or back with your heel from behind. Your opponent is hardly able to defend against this technique, as it is difficult to see. Apideh recalls that this can also lead to a knockout.

Strike with the Palm of the Hand

This technique prevents your opponent from executing a clinch grip. If your opponent attempts to apply a grip, strike the chin with the lower part of your palm. In the process, move your opponent's chin upward and back. For self-defense, the blow can also be aimed to the throat.

Use of the Ropes

Apideh recommends making use of the bouncing action generated by the ropes. When retreating under attack, you must avoid the corners of the ring. If you are close to the center of the rope, take one quick step back and use the momentum of the rope for forward movement. Then carry out an uppercut elbow to your opponent's face. Do not move your elbow upward, but promptly adopt the final position with your shoulder shifting to the front, whereby your opponent cannot hit your face. The power of the move comes from the rebound of the rope and the use of your hip and shoulder.

As an alternative, use the swing of the rope for a quick half circle to the right or left. You will be in a lateral position to your opponent and able to counter with a round kick. For application of this technique in training, make sure the ropes are properly tightened. Apideh used to carry out this particular trick perfectly.

5. Feints

Use feints to mislead your opponent and to tempt him or her to leave a protective stance. Direct the feint to a particular part of the body. As a result your opponent will reduce the protection of another part of the body that can then be attacked effectively with the subsequent technique.

The feint must be swift, and your body must be kept in a relaxed state. If your feint is slow, your opponent will be able to stop the subsequent technique. The feint is frequently carried out as an incomplete move, and your opponent suffers only from little impact. The subsequent technique is then delivered with full power.

Carry out feints at a level or on the side of the body different to the follow-up technique. The aim is that your opponent changes his or her guard, enabling you to attack an unprotected part of the body with a subsequent technique. To this end, focus on the target of the feint and not on the actual target of the follow-up technique.

Not all feints can be carried out easily by all Thai boxers. Test the feints and choose those best suited for your style of fighting. Train in the feints until they become automatic moves. Only a perfect feint will be successful in a fight, which is why you have to repeat previously learned feints time and again and optimize their timing. The feints shown here can be carried out from the front or rear side of the body.

A first selection of feints is introduced here. A comprehensive description can be found in my 2013 book *Muay Thai Training*. You can also see the feints in action on my 2012 DVD *Muay Thai—Technique and Training*.

FEINTS

Feint 1: Leg Kick
Follow-up technique: push kick to the head with the same leg

Feint 2: Several Inside Turns of the Hip
Follow-up technique: round kick

Feint 3: Push Kick
Follow-up technique: front straight punch

Feint 4: Leg Kick
Follow-up technique: round kick to the body or head with the other leg

Competition

Feint 1: Leg Kick

■ **Follow-up technique: push kick to the head with the same leg**

Execution

Out of the fight stance, mislead your opponent to expect a leg kick of your rear leg. In the course of the kick, change the direction of the move and carry out a forward or side kick to the head. Between these moves, your foot does not return to the floor. You can deliver the technique to your opponent's chin or nose.

The technique is usually carried with your rear foot for hard impact and even a knockout. Delivery with the front foot results in a swift impact and serves to prompt the opponent into an uncontrolled attack.

A–D: *Taweesak (left) feints a leg kick with his rear leg. His opponent concentrates on his defense and pulls in his leg for a block. Taweesak changes the direction of the move and hits his head with a push kick.*

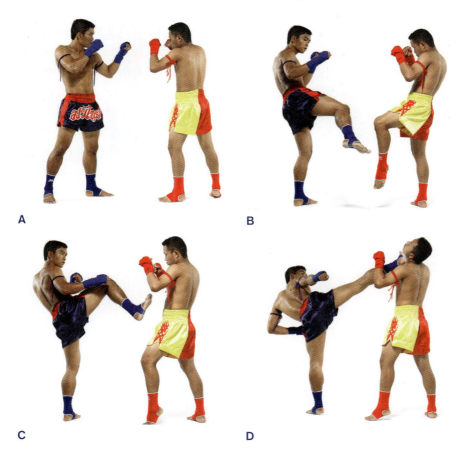

A

B

C

D

Muay Thai Counter Techniques

Feint 2: Several Inside Turns of the Hip
■ Follow-up technique: round kick

Execution

Feint several round kicks by turning your hip in and back out. This will unsettle your opponent, who thus loses timing for a defensive technique, and you can deliver an effective round kick. The move could also prompt your opponent to use an attacking technique that you had been expecting and can now counter effectively.

The turns of the hip as a feint can be carried out with the front and rear leg, but also alternately with both legs.

A–E: *Taweesak (left) feints several round kicks by swiftly turning in his hip. This approach unsettles his opponent, and Taweesak is able to hit his body with a round kick.*

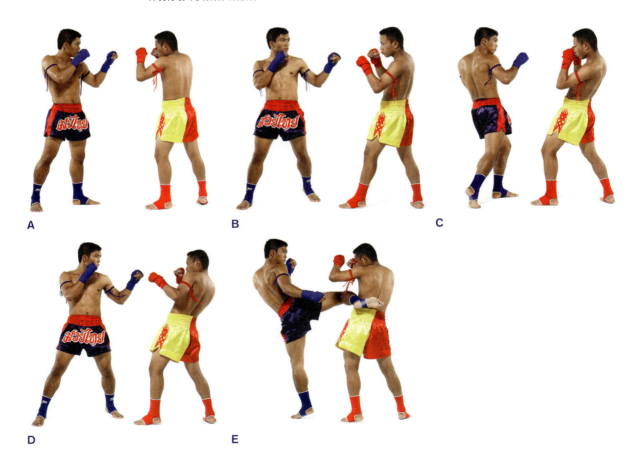

Feint 3: Push Kick

■ Follow-up technique: front straight punch

Execution

In this fight stance, feint a forward kick to the body. In lieu of powerful execution of the kick, quickly put your foot back on the floor in front of you and deliver a straight punch from the front. Shift your weight along with the punch. Insure a quick delivery that surprises and makes your opponent lower the arms for protection. Your opponent can also take a step back and pull in the belly, which will make the head come forward. Both methods of defense make it possible to counter to the head.

A–D: *Taweesak (left) feints a push kick to the body by pulling in his front knee. His opponent pulls in his belly for protection. Taweesak promptly returns his leg to the floor in front and delivers a powerful straight punch to the unprotected head.*

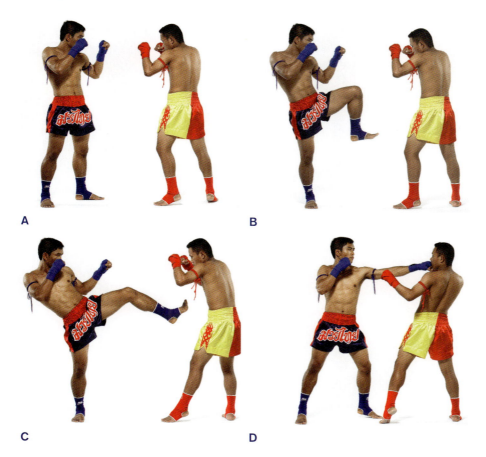

Muay Thai Counter Techniques

Feint 4: Leg Kick

■ Follow-up technique: round kick to the body or head with the other leg

Execution

In the fight stance, feint a knee kick with your front leg. In lieu of powerful execution of the kick, quickly put your leg back on the floor in front and follow with a round kick with the other leg to the body or head. Insure a quick delivery to surprise your opponent, who will attempt defense by pulling the leg back or raising it for a block.

A–C: *Taweesak (left) feints a leg kick with his front leg. His opponent tries to defend himself by pulling his leg back. Taweesak promptly counters with a round kick to his now unprotected body.*

D and E: *Taweesak demonstrates the alternative round kick to the head.*

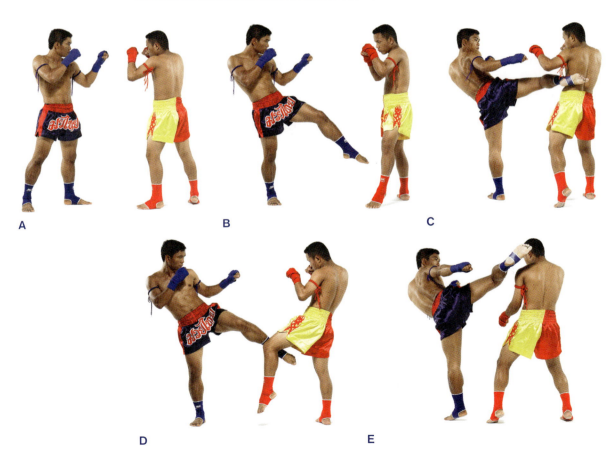

6. Fight Preparation

Ambitious athletic goals demand a detailed training program be worked out to achieve a performance level higher than that of your opponents. There is, however, no program that is valid for all Thai boxers. Rather, you have to determine a program that will satisfy your individual characteristics and requirements.

A training plan with sensible fight preparation for advanced Thai boxers is described here. Thai boxers can also have two daily training sessions six days a week, which requires adequate breaks for recovery. You can use this plan for motivation and adapt it to your individual requirements.

Note that when selecting an individual training program, you have to prepare your body for competition in martial arts and all aspects of fitness, particularly with respect to stamina, power, and speed. Generally speaking, hard and soft training sessions should alternate every other day. The intensity of training is reduced somewhat a few days before the fight. Sparring sessions are left out to avoid injuries. Athletes usually relax on the last day before a competition.

Thai Boxing Training in the Fight Preparation

In the specific training for Thai boxing, the program is tailored to the fight as soon as the opponent is known, and the intensity of training is increased. The trainer determines the fight tactics and chooses the appropriate counter tactics and combinations. If the opponent has excelled as a hard hitter in previous fights, for example, the training will specifically focus on high round kicks to the upper arm. The trainer will urge the athlete to concentrate in pad training on repetitive kicks from varying positions. The repeated

Left to right: the boxer Menny Ossi, several-time Lumpinee champion; Master Chalee; professional referee Mr. Fitzgerald; and Christoph, Rangsit Stadium, Bangkok, Thailand, 1999.

use of knee kicks and push kicks from the opposite side is also suitable in a fight against such an opponent. The athlete has to use these fight tactics over and over until they are known by heart. The sparring partner thus has to imitate the fighting style of the opponent.

Eight-Week Sample Training Program before a Competition

This program shows how advanced amateur Thai boxers lay out a plan for an eight-week training cycle in preparation for a competition. The plan, however, should only be taken as basic information, since individual specifics, such as, for example, weight reduction before a fight, cannot be taken into consideration.

Week 1

Day 1: Muay Thai
Day 2: jogging at medium intensity for 40–60 minutes
Day 3: power training (whole-body program)
Day 4: Muay Thai
Day 5: jogging at low intensity for 40–60 minutes
Day 6: Muay Thai (emphasis on sparring)
Day 7: rest

Week 2

Day 1: Muay Thai
Day 2: interval runs for 40–60 minutes
Day 3: power training (whole-body program)
Day 4: Muay Thai
Day 5: power training (whole-body program); jogging at low intensity for 20–30 minutes
Day 6: Muay Thai (emphasis on sparring)
Day 7: Rest

Week 3

Day 1: Muay Thai
Day 2: interval runs for 40–60 minutes
Day 3: power training (whole-body program)
Day 4: Muay Thai
Day 5: power training (whole-body program); jogging at low intensity for 20–30 minutes
Day 6: Muay Thai (emphasis on sparring)
Day 7: rest

Week 4

Day 1: Muay Thai
Day 2: interval runs (with short sprints) for 40–60 minutes
Day 3: Muay Thai
Day 4: power training (whole-body program)
Day 5: Muay Thai (emphasis on sparring)
Day 6: swimming
Day 7: rest

Week 5

Day 1: Muay Thai (emphasis on competitive tactics)
Day 2: power training (whole-body program)
Day 3: Muay Thai (emphasis on sparring)
Day 4: Muay Thai (emphasis on competitive tactics)
Day 5: interval runs with short sprints for 40–60 minutes
Day 6: Muay Thai (emphasis on sparring)
Day 7: rest

Week 6

Day 1: Muay Thai (emphasis on competitive tactics)
Day 2: interval runs with short sprints for 40–60 minutes
Day 3: power training (whole-body program)
Day 4: Muay Thai (emphasis on sparring)
Day 5: swimming or jogging at low intensity for 40–60 minutes
Day 6: Muay Thai (emphasis on competitive tactics)
Day 7: rest

Week 7

Day 1: Muay Thai (emphasis on sparring)
Day 2: sprint training (sprints over 65 yards, alternating with relaxed jogging)
Day 3: power training (whole-body program)
Day 4: Muay Thai (emphasis on competitive tactics)
Day 5: interval runs for 40 minutes
Day 6: Muay Thai (emphasis on sparring)
Day 7: rest

Week 8

Day 1: Muay Thai (review of competition tactics)
Day 2: shadowboxing (review of competition tactics)
Day 3: jogging at a low heart rate for 30 minutes
Day 4: relaxed shadowboxing
Day 5: rest
Day 6: competition
Day 7: rest

Interval runs are runs for a predetermined period of time at different speeds. Alternate a quick run over a distance of 440 yards, for example, with a very slow jog for some minutes until your heart rate has gone down again. The procedure is repeated a number of times. In the last minutes of the training session, jog at a very slow pace.

A whole-body training made up of eight to ten exercises is recommended for strength training. Reduce the intensity of strength training in the last weeks before the fight. Stick to a healthy diet tailored to your requirements and protein-rich food so that you reach optimal results and minimize the risk of injury and infection.

Extend your sleep cycles for recovery of the body. Other restorative measures are recommended, such as massages and sauna visits at least once a week.

After the competition, take a recreational time-out for a number of days. Light training, such as jogging at low intensity, is resumed after one week at most. Subsequently you can determine a new training cycle.

Christoph (left) and Master Deycha.

Pettapee Por Singtai hits the neck of Woothidet Lukprabat; Pettapee won the match. Lumpinee Stadium, Bangkok, 2000.

Chapter 3
Counters against Fist Techniques

1. Introduction

There are many possible ways to counter fist techniques, and this section outlines frequently used techniques. In addition, techniques are described that are best suited for advanced athletes to supplement their repertoire and to surprise opponents. Choose a selection of counters against all possible attacks, and train in these counters until you succeed in completing them instinctively.

Best suited as a direct counter against a punch are a push kick, side step with a kick, side step with a side hook, or an uppercut elbow. You can dodge an attack by taking a step to the rear or by leaning back with the upper part of your body. You can also deflect a straight punch to the inside or outside, possibly in combination with a side step. You can block a punch up, to the outside, or by turning in the elbow; adopt a stable stance, and promptly follow up with an attacking technique of your own. You can catch straight punches with the palm of your hand while delivering your own straight punch.

Vichan Ponlarit, Fighting name Srisatchanalai Sasriprapayin, was born in 1976. His home is Sukhothai Province. He has had about 127 professional fights, is a former Rajadamnern Champion, and was the Olympic flyweight boxing champion at the 2000 Sydney Games. He ended his active career after his Olympic success.

DIRECT COUNTER

F1: Push Kick

Opponent's technique: all punch techniques

F2: Side Step and Kick

Opponent's technique: straight punch, overhead punch, swing

F3: Uppercut Elbow

Opponent's technique: all punch techniques

F4: Step to the Inside with Side Hook

Opponent's technique: side hook, swing

F5: Side-Bend and Elbow

Opponent's technique: overhead punch

AVOID AND DEFLECT

F6: Step Back

Opponent's technique: all punch techniques

F7: Lean Back

Opponent's technique: all techniques to the head

F8: Lean Back and Dodge

Opponent's technique: powerful straight punch

F9: Deflection to the Inside

Opponent's technique: powerful straight punch

F10: Deflection to the Outside

Opponent's technique: powerful straight punch

F11: Step to the Outside with Deflection

Opponent's technique: straight punch, overhead punch, uppercut

F12: Ducking

Opponent's technique: spinning back fist

F13: Deflection and Wedging In

Opponent's technique: straight punch

Block

F14: Block Upward
Opponent's technique: straight punch

F15: Block to the Outside
Opponent's technique: straight punch, overhead punch, side hook, swing

F16: Arm Block with Inside Turn
Opponent's technique: straight punch

F17: Block against Uppercut
Opponent's technique: uppercut to the body or head

F18: Block against a Punch from the Side
Opponent's technique: side hook, swing

F19: Arm Pushed Down and Elbow
Opponent's technique: rear straight punch, swing, side hook

F20: Block and Spinning Elbow
Opponent's technique: spinning back fist

F21: Block to the Outside and Uppercut Elbow
Opponent's technique: uppercut

Catch

F22: Counterpunch
Opponent's technique: front straight punch in the same stance

2. Direct Counter

F1: Push Kick

■ **Opponent's technique: all punch techniques**

Execution

You can use a push kick to the stomach or thigh against all fist techniques. Kick with your front leg for fast delivery to the target. A kick with your rear leg takes more time, but it enables you to kick with more power. Return your active leg to the floor in front of you after the kick, and follow up with a technique from the rear part of the body. A straight punch or a round kick are suitable counters.

A–D: *Saiyok (right) defends himself with a push kick against an uppercut. He kicks with his front leg to the thigh and follows up with a powerful round kick from the rear.*

A

B

C

D

Counters against Fist Techniques

A–E: *Danthai (right) defends himself against a rear straight punch with a push kick with his rear foot. A subsequent counter from the other side of the body is recommended.*

A

B

C

D

E

F2: Side Step and Kick

■ **Opponent's technique: straight punch, overhead punch, swing**

Execution

In this counter, take a step away from the punch. Step sideways with one leg, and promptly kick with your other leg to the body or thigh. You can move to either the inside or the outside. When moving to the outside, however, you must deflect the punch simultaneously to the inside. It is important to lean sideways with the upper part of your body. Carry out the counter in two rapid consecutive moves: one step with your pivot leg, followed in the next move by a kick with your other leg.

A–D: The opponent attacks with a straight punch. Khunsap (right) defends by moving his left leg to the left, deflects the punch to the right, and promptly delivers a kick with his right leg. An option would be to move his right leg forward to the right, leaning his body to the right and kicking with his left leg.

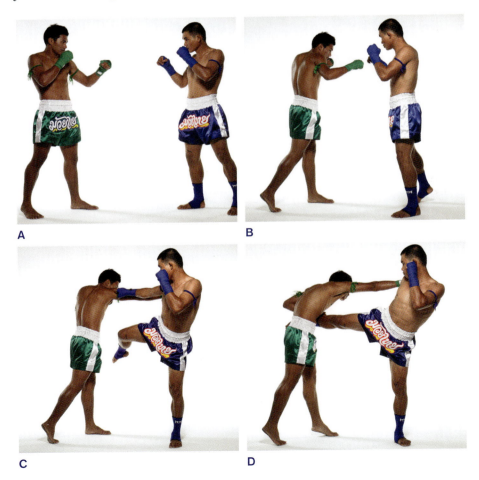

F3: Uppercut Elbow

Opponent's technique: all punch techniques

Execution

The counter can be used against all punch techniques, but it succeeds best against a punch from the side. Defend yourself against the attack by taking a step to the front, turning the upper part of your body forward, and delivering an uppercut elbow. It is important to move forward quickly and in a straight line without hesitation. Follow up with a rotating elbow or a knee kick from the rear.

In this counter you must not initially lower your elbow, as is otherwise standard for an uppercut elbow, but you must move your elbow from the fight stance to the front. Otherwise there is a danger of being hit by your opponent's punch.

A–E: *The opponent attacks with a side hook. Taweesak (left) steps forward with his front foot and delivers an uppercut elbow. To protect his head, he attacks directly out of the fight stance. He promptly follows up with a rotating elbow from the rear.*

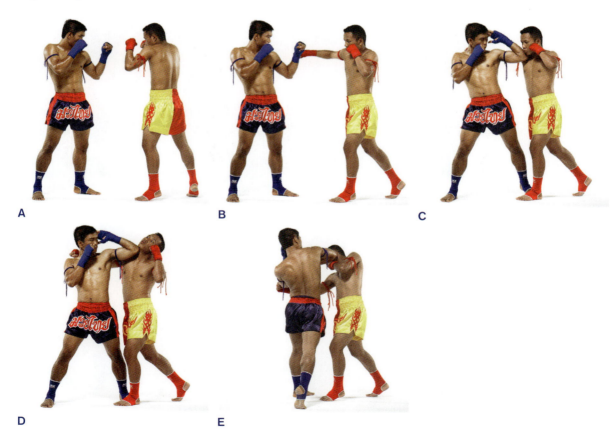

Muay Thai Counter Techniques

F4: Step to the Inside with Side Hook
■ Opponent's technique: side hook, swing

Execution
In this counter, take a step forward with your outer foot while delivering a side hook from the outside. To this end, athletes with a conventional stance must change the stance with a step to the right, southpaws with a step to the left. In direct sequence, you can carry out a rotating elbow with your punching arm.

Concentrate on swift execution, and do not tense the muscles of the arm used for protection. If your opponent's technique impacts first, however, tense the muscles of your arm on the side under attack for a block while guiding your own hook to its target. As an alternative to the side hook, you can also deliver a straight punch or a rotating elbow.

A–D: *The opponent attacks with a right side hook. Christoph (left) counters with a side step and a side hook with his right arm.*

A   B

C   D

Counters against Fist Techniques

F5: Side-Bend and Elbow
■ **Opponent's technique: overhead punch**

Execution

This counter can be used by advanced athletes against a technique from above the head. Take a quick step forward to the outside and duck away sideways, so that the strike misses its target. At the same time, deliver a rotating elbow with your inner arm.

The timing for successful use of this technique requires much training. The technique is extremely effective, however, if it succeeds.

A–D: *The opponent attacks with an overhead punch. Taweesak (left) ducks forward to the left and counters simultaneously with a rotating elbow.*

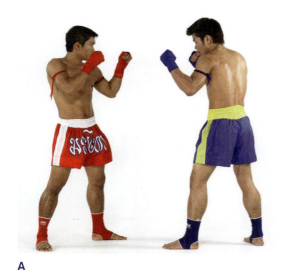

A

B

C

D

3. Avoid and Deflect
F6: Step Back
■ **Opponent's technique: all punch techniques**

Execution

Take a quick step back for defense, so that your opponent's blow misses its target. In the process you can lean back slightly with your upper body. After the miss, your opponent pulls the arm back to the fight position. Move ahead now while delivering a front straight punch. Options are a knee kick or a jumping elbow.

A–D: *The opponent attacks with a front straight punch. Saiyok (left) takes a step back to avoid his opponent's technique, and then promptly counters with a front straight punch.*

Counters against Fist Techniques

F7: Lean Back

■ **Opponent's technique: all techniques to the head**

Execution

In this counter, defend by leaning back with your upper body against a strike to your head. In the course of this move, pull in your chin slightly toward your chest to protect the larynx. Leaning back can also be combined with a swift step to the rear. Having missed the target, your opponent pulls the arm back, enabling you to follow up effectively with a straight punch, an elbow, or a knee kick. When leaning back, be sure to move swiftly and to continue holding up at least one hand for cover.

A–D: *The opponent attacks with a front straight punch. Christoph (left) defends himself by leaning back. He follows up with a straight punch, for which he moves forward with his upper body and brings in his weight.*

A

B

C

D

Muay Thai Counter Techniques

A–D: *Counter against an uppercut from the rear. Taweesak (left) defends himself by leaning back, and he follows up with a powerful straight punch from the rear.*

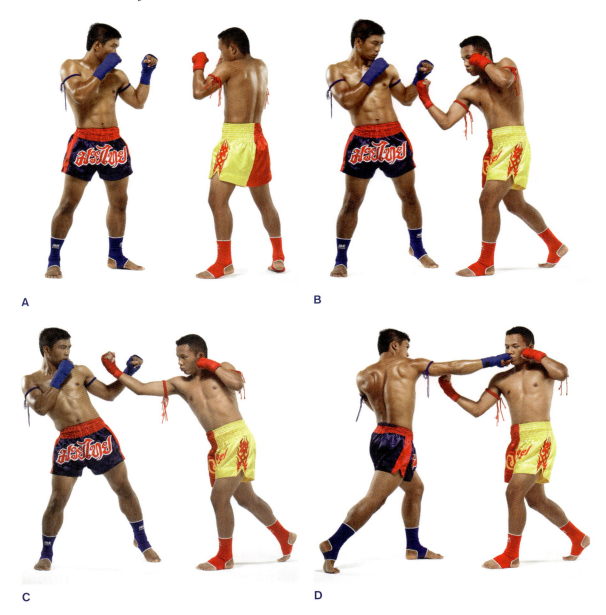

A

B

C

D

Counters against Fist Techniques

F8: Lean Back and Dodge
■ Opponent's technique: powerful straight punch

Execution

This counter can be used by advanced athletes against a powerful straight punch. Initially, lean back with your upper body for cover. Deflect the punch to the inside, and follow with a rotating elbow or an elbow from above. Deliver the strike in the course of a jump, or take a step to the outside, which will reduce the distance to your opponent. Be sure to carry out the leaning back and deflection in direct sequence.

A–E: *The opponent attacks with a powerful straight punch from the rear. Saiyok (left) leans back with his upper body for defense. He then pushes the punch to the inside, jumps up, and makes contact with a rotating elbow.*

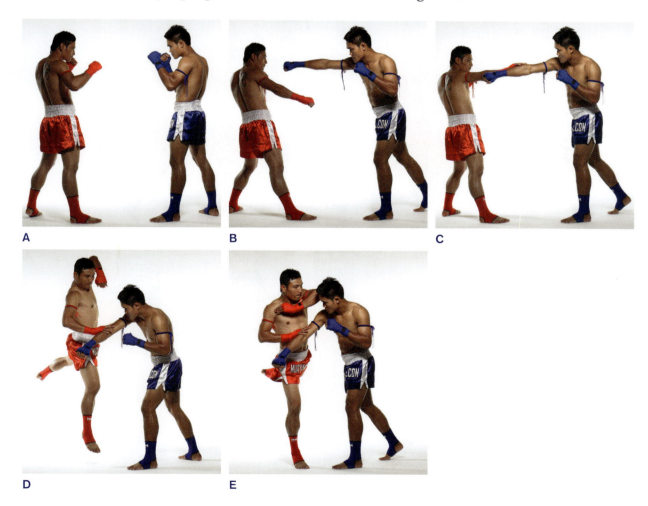

F9: Deflection to the Inside
■ **Opponent's technique: powerful straight punch**

Execution

Deflect your opponent's technique with your opposite hand to the inside while turning the upper side of your body along with it. Follow promptly with a straight punch while turning your upper body back. Keep your body relaxed, and deflect your opponent's arm only slightly to the inside so that you succeed in a fast delivery.

A–D: *The opponent attacks with a rear straight. Christoph (left) deflects the technique to the inside and counters with a straight punch to the unprotected area of the head.*

A   B

C   D

Counters against Fist Techniques

Deflection to the Inside from Different Positions

The technique is also useful if you and your opponent compete in a different fight stance. Deflect your opponent's strike down to the inside with your opposite hand, and follow promptly with a straight punch, a side hook, or an elbow technique. The deflection and the counter are carried out in a swift and consistent move.

A–D: *Christoph (left) has adopted a conventional stance. His opponent attacks with a front straight punch. Christoph deflects the technique to the inside and promptly follows with a side elbow to the now unprotected side of the head.*

A

B

C

D

F10: Deflection to the Outside
■ **Opponent's technique: powerful straight punch**

Execution

This counter can be used by advanced fighters who have developed a good sense of timing. Deflect the punch to the outside, and use your other hand to grab your opponent's inner shoulder. The two moves must be carried out fast and in direct sequence as otherwise your opponent could deliver a technique with the other arm. Next, pull your opponent toward you, and carry out a powerful knee kick.

A–D: *The opponent attacks with a powerful straight punch. Kem (right) deflects the punch to the outside and promptly applies a diagonal grip to the opponent's shoulder. He now pulls in the opponent and delivers a knee kick.*

F11: Step to the Outside with Deflection

■ **Opponent's technique: straight punch, overhead punch, uppercut**

Execution

Take a semicircle step to the outside to avoid the impact of your opponent's strike. At the same time, deflect the strike with your opposite hand to the inside. From a conventional stance, change your stance by taking a step to the right; for southpaws, to the left. As a follow-up technique, you can use an elbow with your front arm. Carry out the deflection and elbow technique in direct sequence, and shift your weight to the front in the process. As an alternative, you can counter with a knee kick from the rear while pulling your opponent toward you.

You can also use this counter against a straight punch or an uppercut to the body. To this end, deflect the strike with your elbow or hand to the inside.

A–D: *Danthai (right) takes an outside step to the front and deflects his opponent's attack with his left hand to the inside. He promptly follows with a rotating elbow.*

A

B

C

D

Muay Thai Counter Techniques

A–D: Rit (right) demonstrates the counter with a knee kick as the follow-up technique. Initially he takes a step forward to the left and deflects the strike to the inside. He then follows up with a knee kick to the open side of the body while pulling in his opponent by the neck. He could also use a round kick if, after the semicircle move, he has gained a bit more distance from the opponent than shown in the photo. If his opponent attacks with a left strike, Rit must move to the right and change his stance. At the same time, he must deflect his opponent's strike to the left.

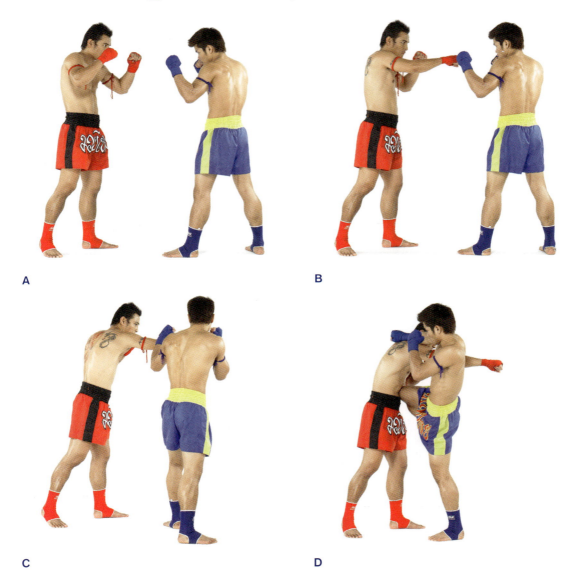

A

B

C

D

Counters against Fist Techniques

A–D: *Armin (right) demonstrates the counter against an uppercut. He takes a forward step to the left and deflects the punch to the inside. The deflection can be carried out with the hand or elbow. He then grabs his opponent and follows up with a knee kick.*

A

B

C

D

F12: Ducking

■ **Opponent's technique: spinning back fist**

Execution

This is a technique for advanced fighters against a spinning back fist. Your opponent starts to deliver the strike out of rotation. Move the upper side of your body to the other side and start to duck away below the strike. If your opponent attacks with a strike from the back of the right hand, duck from left to right. If your opponent uses the left fist instead, move from right to left. After the defense, promptly follow with a straight punch to the unprotected head. As an alternative, advanced fighters can also counter with a lateral knee kick to the head.

The technique is useful against techniques carried out of rotation. On the other hand, in Muay Thai it is very risky to duck below a side hook, as is frequently done in traditional boxing, because your opponent could deliver a knee kick to the head.

A–E: *The opponent attacks with a right spinning back fist; he turns clockwise. Taweesak (left) bends his body to the left continuously by ducking to the right side below his opponent's attack. He promptly follows with a powerful straight punch.*

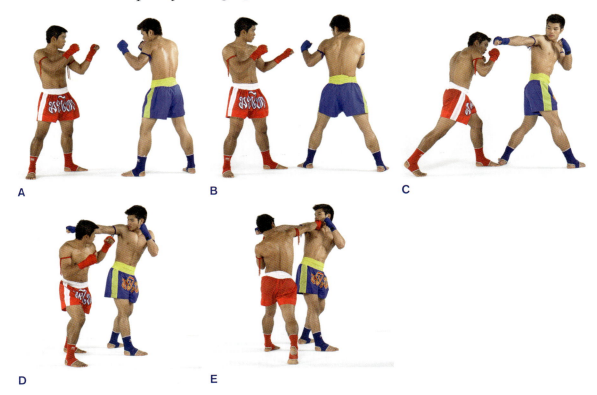

A　　　　　　　　B　　　　　　　　C

D　　　　　　　　E

Counters against Fist Techniques

F13: Deflection and Wedging In
Opponent's technique: straight punch

Execution

This counter is suitable for advanced fighters with a good feel for distance and timing. Deflect your opponent's punch with your opposite hand to the inside while stepping forward to the outside with your foot on the same side. From a conventional stance, you must change your stance with a step to the right; for southpaws with a step to the left. Promptly grab the shoulder from below with your other hand and push your opponent's arm down while leaning with your weight slightly to the side. In direct sequence, deliver your rear knee to the solar plexus or chin.

A–F: *The opponent attacks with a rear straight punch. Taweesak (left) steps forward to the left with his left foot and deflects the punch to the right. He then grabs his opponent's shoulder, pushes him down, and follows up with a knee kick to the chin.*

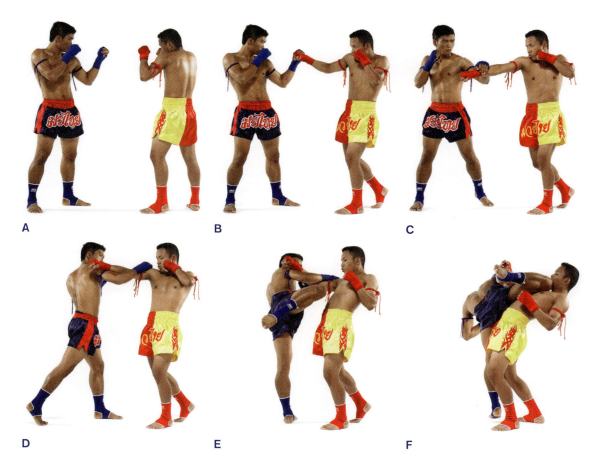

A B C

D E F

Muay Thai Counter Techniques

4. Block

F14: Block Upward

■ **Opponent's technique: straight punch**

Execution

This counter can be used against a powerful straight punch. Block the punch with your opposite lower arm upward. Move your lower arm from below against your opponent's lower arm. Follow up with a knee kick from the same side of your body. Continue holding your opponent's lower arm up so that his or her body is unprotected.

You can also pull in your opponent by the neck before kicking with your rear knee. The pull makes it possible to apply the knee kick with greater force. Performing the technique with your front leg without the pulling action can be carried out faster, however. Put both options to the test, and use the one you consider easier.

A–D: *The opponent attacks with a straight punch from the rear. Taweesak (left) blocks the punch upward. He then follows with a knee kick from the front leg.*

A

B

C

D

Counters against Fist Techniques

F15: Block to the Outside

■ **Opponent's technique: straight punch, overhead punch, side hook, swing**

Execution

In this counter, block with your opposite hand against the upper arm or shoulder of the striking arm. To this end, initially move your hand slightly to the inside in a slightly curving move. Then grab your opponent with your other hand and pull him or her in. Grab with your rear hand from inside around the neck, thereby protecting your head against possible attacks. Follow up promptly with a straight knee kick.

A–D: *The opponent attacks with a straight punch from the rear. Saiyok (left) blocks the punch, pulls his opponent in by the neck, and carries out a knee kick with his rear leg.*

A

B

C

D

Muay Thai Counter Techniques

F16: Arm Block with Inside Turn
■ **Opponent's technique: straight punch**

Execution

In this block, turn your opposite arm to the inside, and move your upper body along with it. Make sure your stance is stable to make a relaxed turn of your body. Follow up with a technique from the other side of your body, such as a straight punch. To this end, turn the upper side of your body back and shift your weight to the front. Options are a follow-up with a rotating elbow or a knee kick from the rear.

A–D: *The opponent attacks with a straight punch. Kem (left) defends himself by turning his body slightly to the right and blocking with his left lower arm. He promptly follows with a powerful straight punch.*

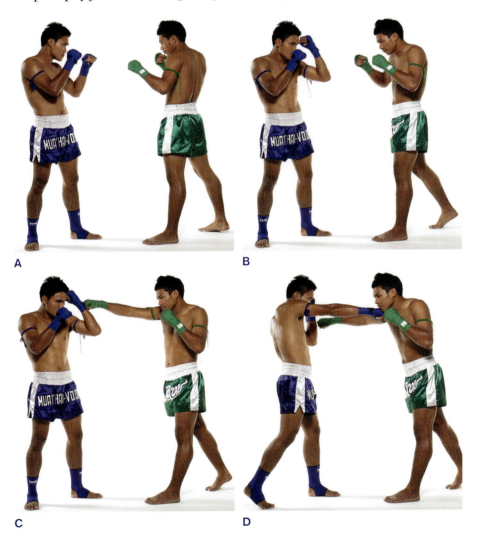

A

B

C

D

Counters against Fist Techniques

F17: Block against Uppercut
■ Opponent's technique: uppercut to the body or head

Execution

This counter can be used against an uppercut. Block the strike with your opposite arm by turning your elbow to the inside. Move along with your body so that the uppercut does not impact at full strength. Follow up promptly with a rotating elbow or a knee kick delivered from the other side of your body. You can stretch your other arm forward to keep your opponent away.

If your opponent aims the uppercut at your chin, turn your elbow in such a way that it protects your chin against an attack from below. For protection against a side hook to the ribs, pull your elbow down to your hip to minimize the area under attack. It is important to follow up with a prompt attacking technique of your own.

A–D: *The opponent attacks with a hook to the body. Danthai (right) blocks the punch and counters with a rotating elbow.*

E: *The arm block from a different perspective.*

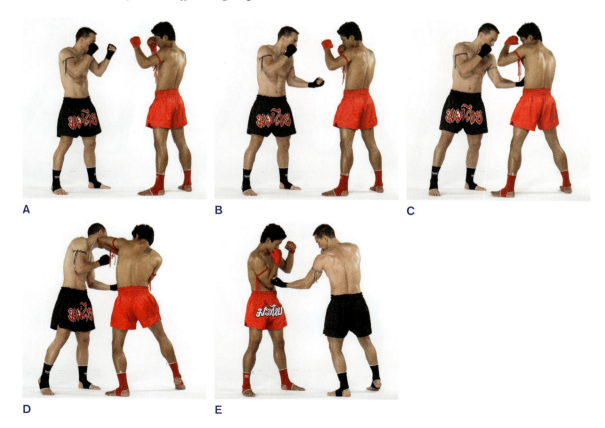

F18: Block against a Punch from the Side

■ **Opponent's technique: side hook, swing**

Execution

Block the punch from the side with your opposite arm. To this end, raise your arm as if you were running your fingers through your hair. At the same time, you can push your opponent away with your other arm. A stable stance is important during the block. Continue with a diagonal grip with your other hand to your opponent's neck. If your opponent aimed the attack at the rear of your body, take an additional jump back with your front leg. Follow up with a powerful knee kick from the rear, for which you pull your opponent toward you. A variant can be an elbow that does not require a previous grip.

A–E: *The opponent attacks with a left side hook. Saiyok (right) blocks with his right, grabs his opponent with his left, and follows up with a knee kick.*

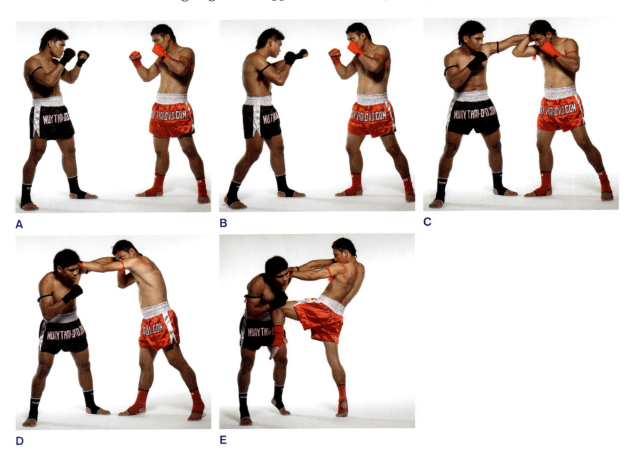

Counters against Fist Techniques

F19: Arm Pushed Down and Elbow
■ **Opponent's technique: rear straight punch, swing, side hook**

Execution

You can use this counter against an opponent's punch from the rear. Step forward with your opposite leg and grab your opponent's upper arm with your arm on the same side. Push your opponent's arm down, and follow up with an elbow of your rear arm with your weight behind it. You can use a rotating elbow with your rear arm, a spear elbow, or an uppercut elbow.

For defense against a straight punch, you have to move your blocking arm forward in a slightly curving move.

A–D: *The opponent attacks with a straight punch from the rear. Taweesak (left) takes a step forward and pushes his opponent's arm down. He then continues with an uppercut elbow.*

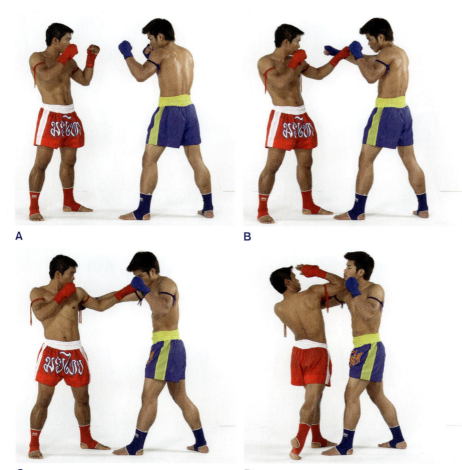

A

B

C

D

Muay Thai Counter Techniques

F20: Block and Spinning Elbow
Opponent's technique: spinning back fist

Execution

This is an effective technique that can be used by advanced athletes, and it is attractive for audiences. Defend yourself against a spinning back fist by taking a step forward and blocking your opponent's punch with both lower arms. If your opponent attacks your right side, move forward with your left leg. Against an attack to your left side, move forward with your right leg. Then turn around on your front foot, and deliver a rotating elbow. In a conventional stance, turn clockwise; for southpaws, turn counterclockwise. In the process, you can move forward with your leg on the active side to achieve a powerful impact.

A–D: *The opponent delivers a spinning back fist. Taweesak (left) blocks the punch and counters with an elbow generated by clockwise rotation.*

Counters against Fist Techniques

F21: Block to the Outside and Uppercut Elbow

▪ **Opponent's technique: uppercut**

Execution

This counter is only suitable for advanced athletes as it requires precise timing. Without proper timing, there is the danger that your opponent's uppercut will slip through your guard.

Use your opposite arm to block the uppercut to the outside by hitting the lower arm down. Continue promptly with a rotating elbow from the other side of your body, and shift your weight to the front. You can subsequently deliver a knee kick from the rear. As a variant, carry out a simultaneous elbow and knee kick from the rear as the follow-up technique.

A–E: *The opponent attacks with an uppercut from the rear. Taweesak (left) blocks the attack to the outside and follows up with a rotating elbow.*

F: *Variant with simultaneous use of an elbow and knee kick.*

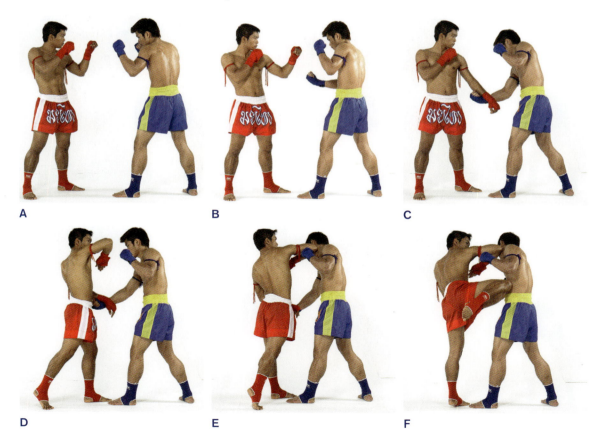

A   B   C

D   E   F

5. Catch
F22: Counterpunch
■ Opponent's technique: front straight punch in the same stance

Execution

Use this counter strike if your opponent delivers a front straight punch from the same stance. Catch the punch with your rear open hand. To this end, push your thumb firmly against the hollow at the base of the biceps of your other arm. Deliver a simultaneous straight punch. The forward stretch of your striking arm and shifting your weight toward your opponent are important. As a variant to the straight punch, you can catch your opponent's punch as before and counter with a side hook or an uppercut.

A–D: *The opponent attacks with a front straight punch. Christoph (left) blocks the technique and counters with a simultaneous front straight punch.*

E: *The technique from a different perspective.*

Nonsai Sor Sanyakorn demonstrates the rotating elbow.
Bangkok, 2012.

Chapter 4
Counters against Elbow Techniques

1. Introduction

Elbow techniques are dangerous and are carried out at close distance. For a successful defense, you must react quickly. Watch out for a firm stance and try to follow your defense with a prompt attack technique.

As direct defense against an elbow technique, it makes sense to use a front straight punch, push kick, or uppercut elbow. You can avoid the elbow technique by taking a step back or leaning back with the upper part of your body. You can also deflect the elbow technique to the inside. To this end, take a step to the outside. For an elbow technique from the front, it is better to dodge. If, however, you are forced to block, hold your arm at an angle. To defend against elbow techniques from the side, push straight in the direction of your lower arm. Carry out the push similar to an uppercut elbow. Try to block the elbow technique before it has reached its full range; that way you do not have to absorb its full impact.

Somkid Kruewaan, fighting names Terdkiat Sitteppitak and Kietrungroj, was born in 1970. His home is in Buriram Province, and his training camp is Kietrungroj Gym in Rayong Province. He has had about 150 professional fights and is a former WMTC champion as well as the Lumpinee champion in the junior featherweight, featherweight, and junior lightweight divisions.

DIRECT COUNTER

E1: Front Straight Punch
Opponent's technique: all elbow techniques

E2: Push Kick
Opponent's technique: all elbow techniques

E3: Uppercut Elbow
Opponent's technique: elbow techniques from the outside or above

E4: Step to the Inside with Side Elbow
Opponent's technique: all elbow techniques

E5: Side Step and Knee Kick
Opponent's technique: all elbow techniques

AVOID AND DEFLECT

E6: Step Back
Opponent's technique: all elbow techniques

E7: Lean Back
Opponent's technique: elbow techniques to the head

E8: Step to the Outside and Deflection
Opponent's technique: uppercut elbow, spear elbow, rotating elbow

BLOCK

E9: Block and Elbow
Opponent's technique: reverse elbow

E10: Block against Elbow from the Front
Opponent's technique: uppercut elbow, spear elbow, elbow from above

E11: Block against Elbow from the Side
Opponent's technique: rotating elbow, side elbow

E12: Block and Rotating Elbow
Opponent's technique: rotating elbow, side elbow

E13: Block and Diving
Opponent's technique: spinning elbow

Counters against Elbow Techniques

2. Direct Counter

E1: Front Straight Punch

■ **Opponent's technique: all elbow techniques**

Execution

In this counter, use a front straight punch to stop your opponent's attack. To this end, you can take a small step forward. It is important that you move promptly forward without hesitation. In addition, you must stretch your arm and put your weight behind the hit. Follow up with an elbow or knee kick from the rear part of your body.

When training, slightly push with the palm of your hand to the chest to avoid injury.

A–D: *Saiyok (right) defends against an uppercut elbow by taking a step forward with a simultaneous front straight punch. He promptly follows with a rotating elbow from the rear.*

A

B

C

D

E2: Push Kick

■ **Opponent's technique: all elbow techniques**

Execution

A push kick can be used against all possible elbow techniques; your opponent will be put off-balance, and the attack will be stopped. Rest your kicking leg on the floor in front of you and follow up with a straight punch, elbow, round, or knee kick, depending on your distance from your opponent.

The push kick can be carried out with the front or rear leg. The front leg will impact faster, while the rear leg can be more powerful. Practice both alternatives in training so that the suitable technique can be used in a fight situation.

A–E: *The opponent attacks with a rotating elbow. Nonsai (left) defends with a push kick to the leg. He promptly follows up with a knee kick from behind.*

Counters against Elbow Techniques

E3: Uppercut Elbow

■ **Opponent's technique: elbow techniques from the outside or above**

Execution

For this counter, use an uppercut elbow as defense. Take a step forward, and put your weight behind the hit. The prompt action out of the fight stance without previously lowering your arm is important. It's best to place the palm of your hand on your head for protection if the opponent's elbow should impact first. Follow up with a rotating elbow carried out by your other arm.

A–D: *The opponent attacks with a spear elbow. Danthai (right) defends with an uppercut elbow of his opposite arm and follows up with a rotating elbow.*

A

B

C

D

Muay Thai Counter Techniques

Uppercut Elbow against a Spinning Elbow

You can also use an uppercut elbow as defense against a spinning elbow. Be sure that your weight is shifted to the front. If you move laterally to the outside instead to get away from your opponent's technique, you will be slower and exert only a little impact.

If your opponent's technique impacts first, block by tensing your other arm, and don't interrupt your own elbow technique.

A–D: *The opponent attacks with a spinning elbow, for which he turns clockwise. Rit (right) defends himself with an uppercut elbow. His opponent moves far to the front, so that Rit does not have to take a forward step.*

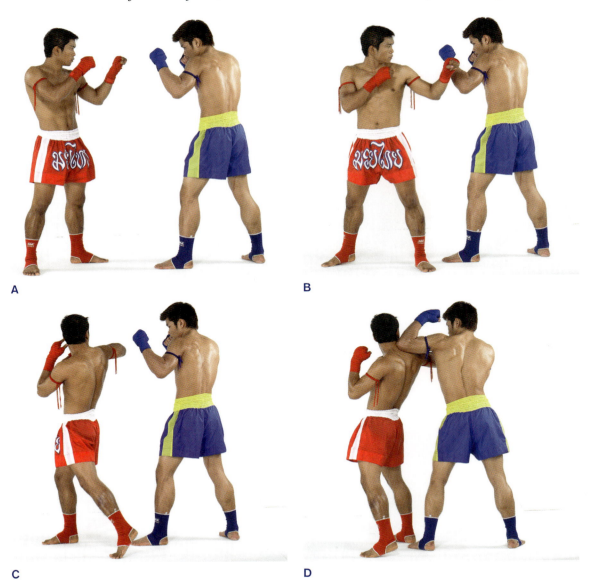

Counters against Elbow Techniques

E4: Step to the Inside with Side Elbow
■ Opponent's technique: all elbow techniques

Execution

In this counter, defend with a semicircle to the inside so that you assume a sideways position to your opponent, whose technique will miss its target. From a conventional stance, change that stance with a step to the right; southpaws with a step to the left. At the same time, deliver a rotating elbow. The elbow impacts on the return of the foot to the floor, thereby insuring powerful execution. Options are an uppercut elbow or a spear elbow.

A–C: *The opponent attacks with an uppercut elbow carried out with the right arm. Saiyok (left) takes a side step to the right and delivers a rotating elbow in the process. If his opponent hits with his left arm, however, Saiyok must make a half circle to the left and use his left elbow.*

A B C

Muay Thai Counter Techniques

E5: Side Step and Knee Kick
■ **Opponent's technique: all elbow techniques**

Execution

Defend against the elbow technique with a side step away from the attack. Move your outer foot farther to the outside, and deliver a kick to the body with your inner knee. It is important to carry out the counter in two steps: initially, the step with the outer foot, promptly followed by the knee kick. If your opponent's kick impacts first, block with your lower arms held up.

A–D: *The opponent attacks with a right elbow. Khunsap (right) moves his right foot forward and kicks in the process with his left knee to the stomach. Additionally, he pulls his opponent slightly toward him with his inner hand.*

A

B

C

D

Counters against Elbow Techniques

3. Avoid and Deflect
E6: Step Back

■ **Opponent's technique: all elbow techniques**

Execution

With a step or jump back, you can defend against all elbow techniques. You can also lean back slightly with your upper body. Follow up with a hitting technique from the rear, simultaneously moving ahead again. Options are counters with a kicking or jumping technique.

To be sure of success with these counters, you must be very quick. Pay attention to shifting your weight forward in the subsequent technique.

A–D: *The opponent attacks with a side elbow. Saiyok (left) takes a step back, so that the elbow technique misses its target. He promptly counters with a rear straight punch.*

A

B

C

D

Muay Thai Counter Techniques

A–E: *The opponent attacks with a jumping elbow technique. Taweesak (left) takes a wide step back and follows up with a jumping knee kick.*

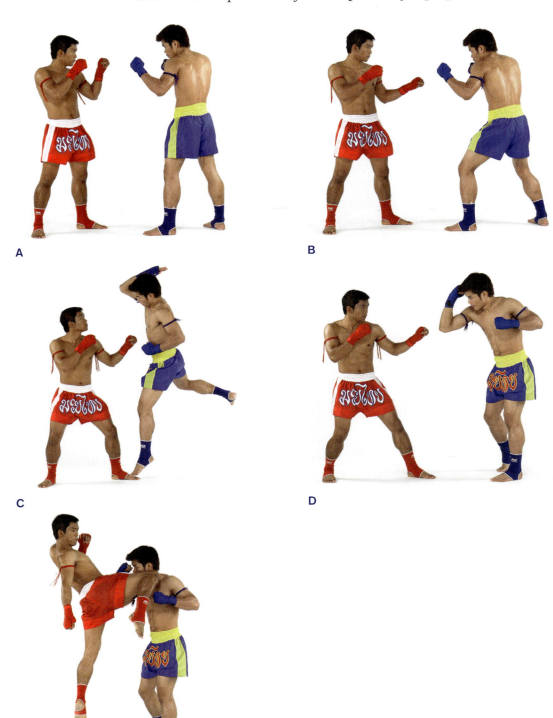

A

B

C

D

E

Counters against Elbow Techniques

E7: Lean Back
Opponent's technique: elbow techniques to the head

Execution

In this counter, defend by leaning your upper body back. In the process, pull your chin slightly toward your chest to protect the larynx. You can also combine the motion of leaning back with a quick step back. Promptly continue with an elbow technique or a punch from the rear while moving forward with your weight behind the technique. Advanced athletes can counter with a kick to the head or a knee kick while pulling the opponent in. When leaning back, be sure to keep at least one hand up for cover.

A–D: *The opponent attacks with a rotating elbow. Saiyok (left) dodges the attack by leaning back and continues with a rotating elbow.*

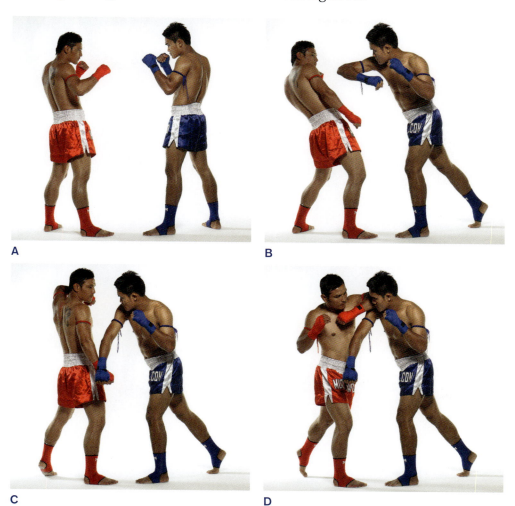

A

B

C

D

Muay Thai Counter Techniques

A–D: *The opponent attacks with an uppercut elbow. Danthai (right) leans back so that the attack misses its target. He promptly follows up with a straight punch to the body. At that distance, options are a straight punch to the head, an elbow, or a knee kick.*

A

B

C

D

E8: Step to the Outside and Deflection

■ **Opponent's technique:** uppercut elbow, spear elbow, rotating elbow

Execution

In this counter, avoid the elbow technique by moving a half circle to the outside. In the process, deflect the attack to the inside with your opposite hand. In a conventional stance, change that stance with a step to the right; southpaws with a step to the left. Promptly follow up with a rotating elbow carried out by the same arm. Alternatively, you can use an elbow from above with your rear arm. Be sure that you carry out the deflection and the elbow technique in direct sequence.

A–D: *Taweesak (left) defends himself against an uppercut elbow by deflecting the elbow to the inside and at the same time taking a step to the left. He promptly follows up with a rotating elbow. If, however, his opponent hits with his left arm, Taweesak must do a half circle to the right with a change in his stance.*

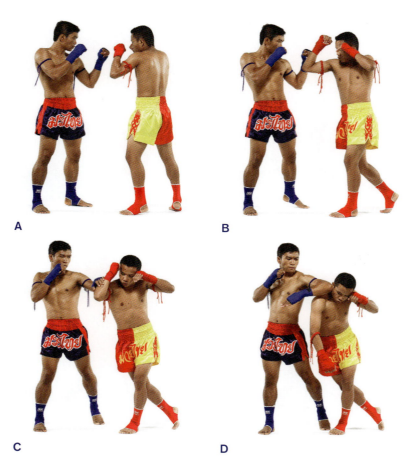

A   B

C   D

Muay Thai Counter Techniques

4. Block
E9: Block and Elbow
Opponent's technique: reverse elbow

Execution

Use this counter whenever your opponent attacks with a reverse elbow. Your opponent can either turn in his or her body directly in order to create pretension for the rear elbow, or use the reverse elbow if the side elbow or rotating elbow has missed its target. Block the rear elbow with your opposite arm. You can subsequently deliver an elbow from above with your other arm.

A–D: *The opponent misses his target with a lateral elbow technique as Taweesak (left) is leaning back. Taweesak then blocks the subsequent reverse elbow and counters with a jumping elbow.*

A

B

C

D

Counters against Elbow Techniques

E10: Block against Elbow from the Front

■ **Opponent's technique:** uppercut elbow, spear elbow, elbow from above

Execution

For this counter, block an elbow technique from above or below by holding your lower arm sideways. Move forward in the process and block toward the center of your arm, thus absorbing only a little of the potential impact. Follow up with an elbow or a knee kick from the other side of the body. As a variant, block an elbow from above with your lower arms held crosswise, thereby stabilizing your position, before following with a knee kick.

A–E: *The opponent attacks with an elbow. Taweesak (left) blocks the technique and delivers a knee kick. When his foot returns to the floor, he follows up with a rotating elbow.*

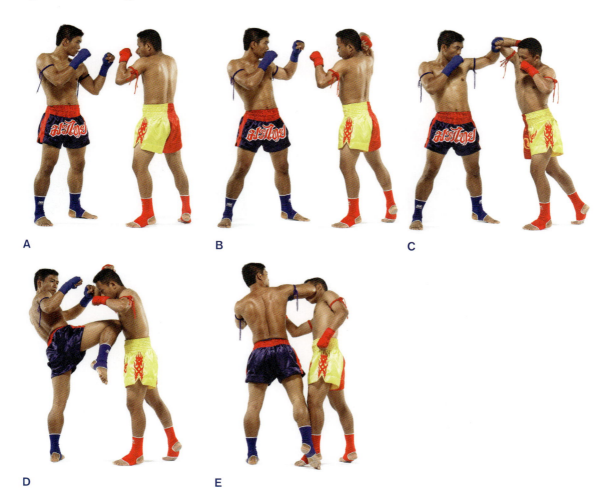

A B C

D E

Muay Thai Counter Techniques

A–D: *You can also block a front uppercut elbow with the inside of your front glove, followed up by a prompt elbow with the same arm. By the same token, it is important to move toward your opponent in order to block the attack before the entire range of the move is complete, so that it does not impact with full force.*

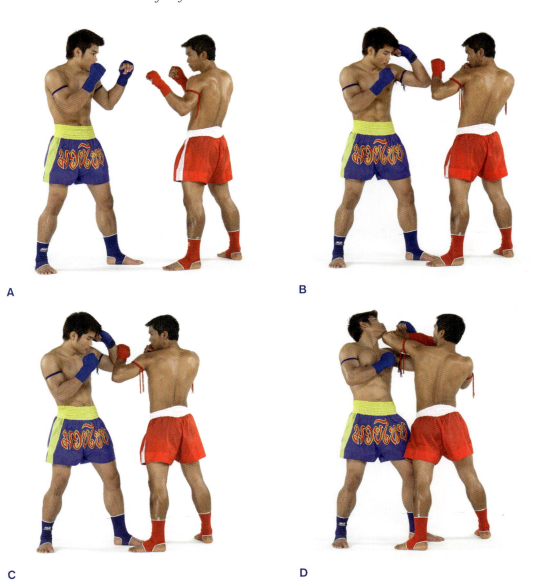

A

B

C

D

E11: Block against Elbow from the Side
■ Opponent's technique: rotating elbow, side elbow

Execution

Block the elbow technique from outside to the center of your lower arm. Carry out the block similar to an uppercut elbow while placing your hand on your forehead to stabilize the position. Promptly counter with a knee kick or an elbow from the other side of the body. It is important to block into your opponent's attack, and to move forward and maintain a firm stance.

A–D: *The opponent attacks with a rotating elbow. Danthai (right) blocks the technique and follows with a knee kick from behind, for which he pulls in his opponent.*

Muay Thai Counter Techniques

A–D: *The opponent attacks with a rotating elbow. Rit (left) blocks and follows with an uppercut elbow from behind.*

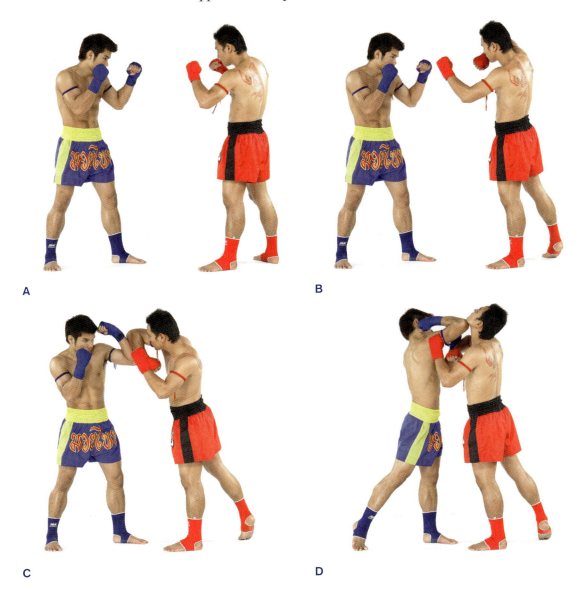

A

B

C

D

Counters against Elbow Techniques | 97

E12: Block and Rotating Elbow
■ **Opponent's technique: rotating elbow, side elbow**

Execution

The opponent attacks with an elbow technique from the side. Block the technique with your lower arm on the same side of the body while moving your leg forward. Quickly turn on this leg. In a southpaw stance, rotate counterclockwise. Use the momentum of the turn to deliver your rear elbow to the target. In the process, you can move your leg on the active side forward, but this is not absolutely necessary. You can deliver either sideways to the jaw or from below to the chin.

A–E: *Taweesak (left) blocks a rotating elbow with his rear arm. To this end, he moves his rear foot ahead. He then turns counterclockwise and follows up with an elbow while turning.*

A   B

C   D   E

Muay Thai Counter Techniques

E13: Block and Diving
■ **Opponent's technique: spinning elbow**

Execution
This counter is useful for advanced athletes who want to broaden their repertoire with a spectacular technique.

Defend against a spinning elbow with a block, which requires taking a step forward. In contrast to the previous E12 technique, block with your opposite arm. If your opponent attacks your right side, block with your right arm and move your right leg forward. If, however, your opponent attacks your left side, block with your left arm and move your left leg forward. After the block, bend your body, and turn with your back toward your opponent. At the same time, carry out a rear elbow with your other arm.

A–D: *The opponent uses an elbow while turning. Taweesak (left) blocks the technique with his right arm and moves his right leg forward in the process. He then dives and turns counterclockwise in order to deliver an elbow from below.*

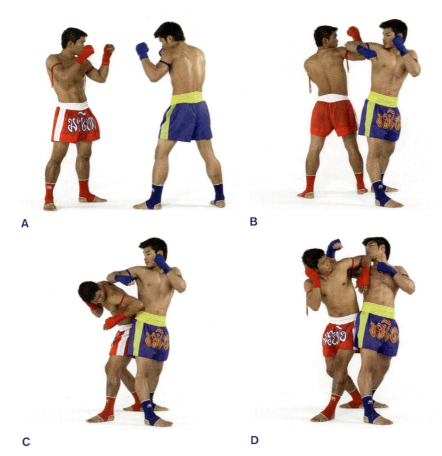

A   B

C   D

Saiyok demonstrates the round kick.
Bangkok, 2012.

Chapter 5

Counters against Kicking Techniques

1. Introduction

Powerful kicks are characteristic of Muay Thai. Kicks are a spectacular sight, and they can result in an early end to a fight regardless of whether they are delivered to the leg, body, or head. It is possible to defend against fighters with excellent kick techniques and to counter effectively, and to do so, you must learn a variety of techniques. Continue to train to perfection in the counters you choose so that they succeed in a fight.

Direct counters against kicks can be a straight punch, a push kick, a kick to the pivot leg, an elbow to the kicking leg, and a side step with a punch. When hit with a direct counter, your opponent will be put off-balance, and depending on the distance between you, you can continue with another attacking technique. You can dodge kick attacks by taking a step back, leaning back, or pulling your leg back. This will also place your opponent in a disadvantageous fight situation and enable you to counter with a powerful attacking technique. A kick to the leg or body can be blocked with the shin. For that kind of block, it is important to maintain a stable stance and to pull your knee up in a rapid motion while not lowering the arms. If you succeed in catching the kicking leg, you can attack your opponent effectively with your knee or elbow, delivering the attack to the body or the kicking leg. Additionally, your opponent could fall after a kick or sweep to the pivot leg. If your opponent attempts to catch your kick, you can defend with a straight punch, holding or forcing your leg out of the grip.

Direct Counter

S1: Front Straight Punch
Opponent's technique: round kick to the leg, body, or head

S2: Push Kick
Opponent's technique: all round kicks, spinning heel kick

S3: Kick to the Inner Leg
Opponent's technique: high round kick

S4: Elbow Hit to the Thigh
Opponent's technique: round kick to the body

S5: Step to the Inside with Side Hook
Opponent's technique: round kick

S6: Side Step
Opponent's technique: heel kick from above

Avoid and Deflect

S7: Step Back
Opponent's technique: round kick

S8: Lean Back
Opponent's technique: kick to the head, spinning heel kick

S9: Pull the Leg Back
Opponent's technique: kick to the inside of the leg

Block

S10: Block and Attack
Opponent's technique: leg kick, round kick to the body

S11: Knee Block and Elbow Hit
Opponent's technique: round kick to the body or head

Catch

S12: Catch and Attack
Opponent's technique: round kick to the body or thigh

S13: Attack of a Caught Leg
Opponent's technique: round kick to the body or thigh

S14: Catch and Kick against the Pivot Leg
Opponent's technique: round kick to the body

S15: Catch and Sweep
Opponent's technique: round kick to the body

S16: Catch and Turn In
Opponent's technique: round kick to the body

Defense against Catch

S17: Straight Punch against a Catch
Opponent's technique: catching a round kick

S18: Turn of the Hip and Elbow Hit
Opponent's technique: catching a round kick

S19: Twisting the Leg Out
Opponent's technique: catching a round kick

2. Direct Counter
S1: Front Straight Punch
■ **Opponent's technique:** round kick to the leg, body, or head

Execution

A front straight punch is an effective counter against all round kicks. Move forward with your front foot while delivering a front straight punch. Then shift your weight to the front and stretch your arm and your body. Your opponent is put off-balance due to the punch, and the kicking motion is stopped. Subsequently, follow up with an elbow, knee kick, or a kick from the rear side of your body.

The counter can be used against kicks from the right and left. In training, don't strike the face, but push the palm of your hand slightly to the chest to avoid injury.

A–D: *Christoph (left) defends against a round kick by taking a step forward while delivering a front straight punch.*

E: *The technique against a round kick with the left leg.*

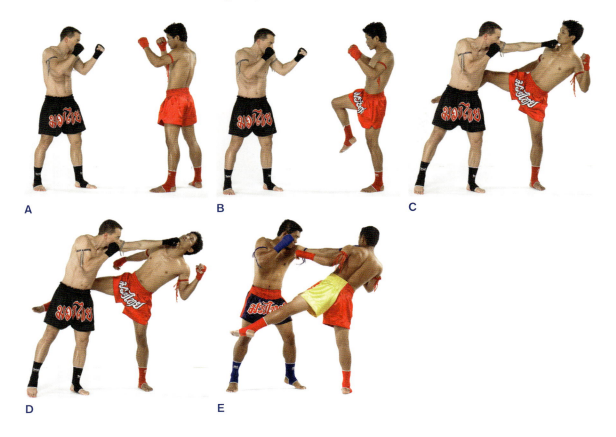

Counters against Kicking Techniques

S2: Push Kick

■ **Opponent's technique: all round kicks, spinning heel kick**

Execution

A push kick can be used against all kicks from the side. Kick to the stomach, pivot leg, or thigh of the active leg. Your opponent will thus be put off-balance, and the kicking motion is stopped. Rest your kicking leg in front of you, and follow up with a straight punch, elbow, round kick, or knee kick.

You can carry out the push kick with your front or rear leg. With your front leg, the impact will be quicker, while your rear leg will be more powerful. Practice both sides in training so that the most suitable technique will come instinctively in a fight situation.

A–E: *Danthai (right) defends himself with a push kick to the thigh. He then returns his kicking leg to the floor in front of him and continues with a rotating elbow from the rear.*

Muay Thai Counter Techniques

A–D: *The opponent attacks with a round kick with his right leg. Danthai (right) defends himself with a push kick with his rear leg. He returns his kicking leg to the floor in front of him, which enables him to use his left arm for a rear straight.*

E: *The push kick against a spinning heel kick. Kick toward the opponent's lower back.*

Counters against Kicking Techniques

S3: Kick to the Inner Leg
■ Opponent's technique: high round kick

Execution

This counter can be used against a high kick. Defend yourself by taking a step away from the kick with your outer leg, and kick with your inner leg to the back of your opponent's knee or the lower leg. Be sure that your body and leg are leaning away from your opponent's kick for protection.

A–C: *The opponent attacks with a high round kick carried out with the right leg. Saiyok (right) moves his right leg to the right and kicks with his left leg toward the back of the knee.*

D: *The counter against a kick with the left leg. Saiyok moves his left leg to the outside and kicks with his right toward the lower leg.*

A

B

C

D

S4: Elbow Hit to the Thigh
■ **Opponent's technique: round kick to the body**

Execution

In this counter, carry out an elbow technique against the kicking leg. Hit the center of the thigh with your elbow on the same side of the body. When hitting with the rear elbow, slightly advance the rear leg. It is now possible to follow up with a rotating elbow or a knee kick.

Advanced athletes can use a spinning elbow as a follow-up technique. To this end, turn quickly on your front leg. If you are in a southpaw stance, rotate counterclockwise, and vice versa. Deliver the spinning rear elbow to the jaw or chin from below.

A–E: *Taweesak (left) defends himself with an elbow to the thigh. In the process, he moves his rear leg forward. He then turns on this leg and follows with a spinning elbow.*

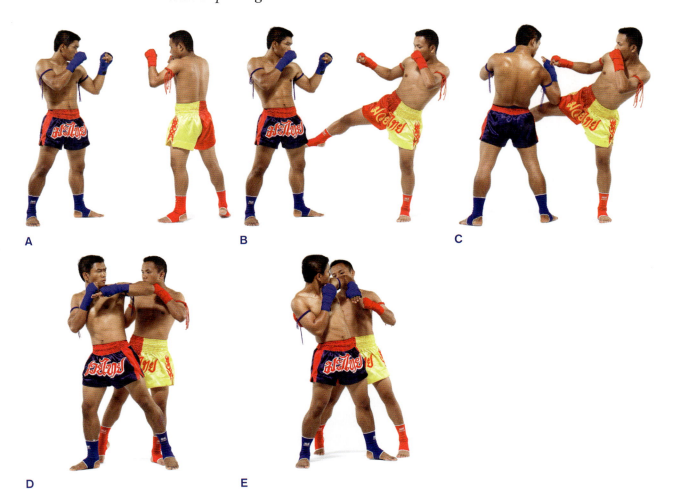

S5: Step to the Inside with Side Hook
■ Opponent's technique: round kick

Execution

The half-circle step with a side hook is an effective counter against all round kicks. Take a step forward to the outside with your outer leg. In the process, deliver a side hook with your outer arm. In the conventional stance, take a step to the right; a southpaw takes a step to the left. The impact of the side hook should now come when your foot returns to the floor, and your weight should be behind the delivery. Subsequently, you can follow up with a rotating elbow of the same arm or a knee kick from the rear.

A–D: *The opponent attacks with a right kick to the head. Khunsap (right) takes a step forward to the outside and counters with a simultaneous side hook.*

A

B

C

D

Muay Thai Counter Techniques

A–E: *Kem (right) demonstrates the counter against an attack with the left. He takes a step forward to the left outside and delivers a side hook. He continues promptly with a rotating elbow.*

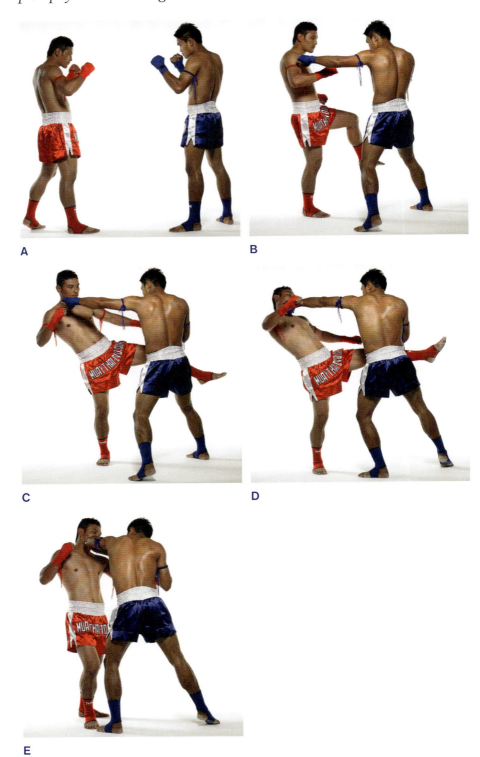

A

B

C

D

E

Counters against Kicking Techniques

S6: Side Step

Opponent's technique: heel kick from above

Execution

Use this counter against a heel kick from above. Defend yourself with a step away from the kick and deliver a side hook or a straight punch with your outer arm. If your opponent pulls his leg up from the inside, move outside. If your opponent raises the leg from the outside, however, take a step to the inside. In a conventional stance, change the stance with a step to the right; a southpaw steps to the left. Be sure to put your weight behind the punch. You can follow up with an elbow technique or a knee kick.

A–D: *The opponent attacks with a heel kick. In the process, he moves his attacking leg from the inside out. Rit (right) takes a step forward to the right with a change of stance and delivers a simultaneous punch to the target.*

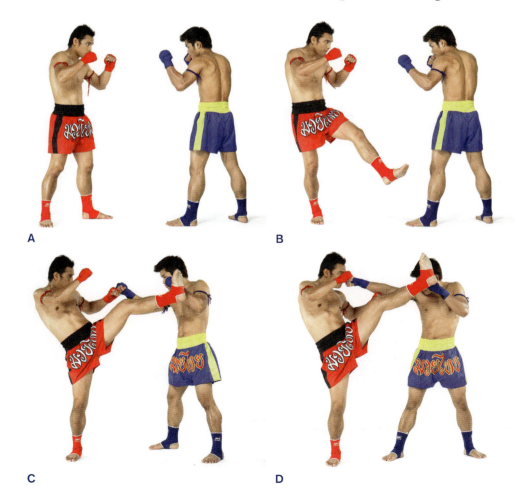

A

B

C

D

3. Avoid and Deflect
S7: Step Back
■ **Opponent's technique: round kick**

Execution

Defend against a round kick with a large step or jump back. A kick to the body can be deflected to the side, causing the opponent to be put off-balance. Be sure to carry out the deflection in a steady motion. Then move ahead again and follow up with a powerful technique, such as a round kick from the rear.

Alternatively, you can follow up with a knee kick or a jump technique. In addition, for defense against a high kick, you can take a step back or lean your head back.

A–E: *The opponent attacks with a right kick to the body. Danthai (right) takes a step back and deflects the kick to the outside. He then follows with a kick to the body. If, however, his opponent kicks with his left leg, it would make sense for Danthai to deliver a kick with his rear leg to the back of the knee.*

A   B

C   D   E

S8: Lean Back

■ **Opponent's technique: kick to the head, spinning heel kick**

Execution

In this counter, lean back with your upper body so that your opponent's attack misses its target. To this end, take your rear foot back. Be sure to pull your chin slightly toward your chest for protection of the larynx. Leaning back can also be done in connection with a step to the rear. Select the follow-up technique depending on the distance to your opponent. A follow-up is best delivered with the rear side of the body.

A–E: *The opponent attacks with a high kick. Christoph (left) leans back with his upper body and counters with a round kick to the body.*

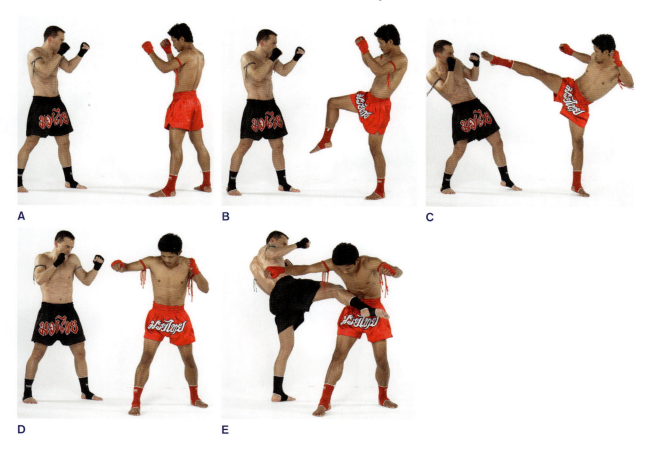

Muay Thai Counter Techniques

S9: Pull the Leg Back
■ Opponent's technique: kick to the inside of the leg

Execution

You can use this counter if your opponent attacks the front inside of your leg. Pull your leg back in a semicircular motion so that your opponent's kick misses its target. To enable a rapid move, turn your upright body along with a snappy move. Follow up with a round or knee kick using the leg that has been pulled back.

It is risky to apply the technique against a kick to the outside of the leg, as your opponent may possibly hit your pivot leg.

A–E: *The opponent attacks with a kick to the inside of the leg. Christoph (left) pulls back the leg under attack and then counters with a round kick.*

4. Block

S10: Block and Attack

▪ **Opponent's technique: leg kick, round kick to the body**

Execution

Block a round kick with your opposite shin. Raise your blocking leg depending on the height of your opponent's kick. In the case of a body kick, move it up to your elbow. Next, briefly step back on the floor and promptly follow with a round kick. For the block, it is important to take on a stable stance and to raise your leg swiftly.

As an option, rest your leg on the floor in front of you and follow up with a punch, knee kick, or kick from the other side of the body.

A–E: *The opponent attacks with a round kick to the body. Danthai (right) blocks the technique, briefly returns his foot to the floor, and finally follows with a round kick.*

Muay Thai Counter Techniques

A–E: *Danthai demonstrates the block against a leg kick. He briefly steps on the floor and follows with a round kick to this leg. As an alternative, you can rest your leg on the floor in front of you and follow with a technique from the rear.*

A

B

C

D

E

Counters against Kicking Techniques

S11: Knee Block and Elbow Hit
■ Opponent's technique: round kick to the body or head

Execution

In this counter, block with your knee to the thigh of the kicking leg. Start with a straight knee and turn your leg in order to be able to hit the center of the thigh. At the same time, start to deliver a rotating elbow that impacts on the return of the kicking leg to the floor in front of you.

Advanced athletes can follow with a spinning elbow. To this end, perform a quick turn on your front leg. In a conventional stance, you turn clockwise; as a southpaw, counterclockwise. Use the momentum gained by the rotation to deliver the rear elbow laterally to the jaw or from below to the chin. During the move, you can rest the leg of the active side in front of you, but this is not absolutely necessary.

A–F: *Taweesak (left) blocks the round kick with a knee. When returning his leg to the floor, he follows with a rotating elbow. He then turns counterclockwise on his front leg to enable delivery of a spinning elbow.*

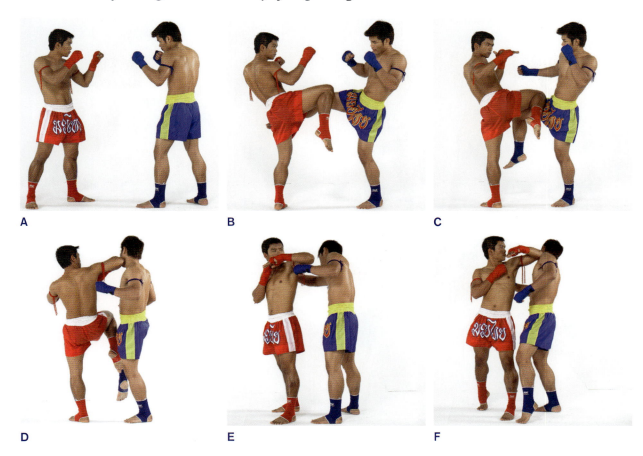

A   B   C

D   E   F

5. Catch

S12: Catch and Attack

■ **Opponent's technique: round kick to the body or thigh**

Execution

In this counter, catch the round kick and attack your opponent with a technique of your own. Take a step to the outside to catch the leg and hold it firmly below your armpit. Next, raise it slightly or turn it down, so that your opponent is put off-balance. Your other arm moves initially to your face and then promptly from the inside to your opponent's neck. Due to the diagonal grip, protect your head against punch techniques. Pull your opponent toward you and carry out a knee technique. As an option, you can follow with a straight punch or elbow from the rear.

If the application of this technique is misjudged, it always entails the risk that your opponent's technique finds your ribs. Your opponent could also deliver a straight punch with the same arm, which is why your other hand should always guard your face.

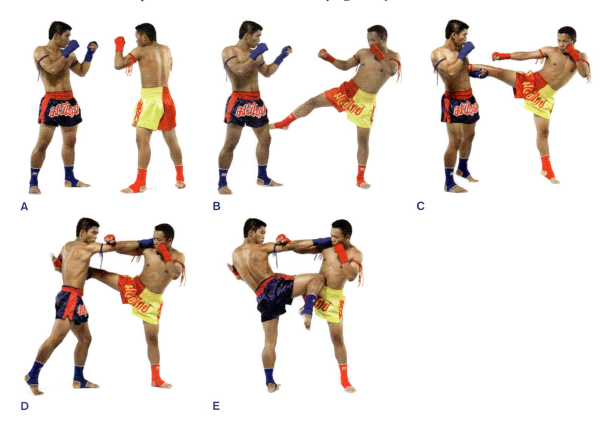

Counters against Kicking Techniques

A–E: The opponent attacks with a round kick to the body. Taweesak (left) takes a step away from the kick while catching his leg. He is now able to control his opponent, pull him in, and attack with a knee kick.

A–D: The opponent carries out a round kick to the body. Rit (right) takes a step away from the kick and catches his leg. He quickly raises the leg slightly and follows with an uppercut elbow, for which he moves forward.

A

B

C

D

Muay Thai Counter Techniques

S13: Attack of a Caught Leg
■ **Opponent's technique: round kick to the body or thigh**

Execution

In this counter, catch a round kick and follow up by attacking the kicking leg. Take a step to the outside to catch your opponent's leg and hold it firmly below your armpit. Your other arm is held in front of your face for protection. Raise the leg slightly to be able to control your opponent. Then deliver a powerful elbow to the thigh. As an option, you can attack the kicking leg with knee kicks while pushing your opponent away.

Leg catching always entails the risk that, when misjudged, your opponent's kick can hit your ribs. The technique must therefore be trained in to perfection before it can be used instinctively in a fight.

A–D: *Taweesak (left) takes a step to the right and catches the round kick. He pulls the leg slightly up, causing his opponent to be put off-balance, and continues with an elbow from above to the thigh.*

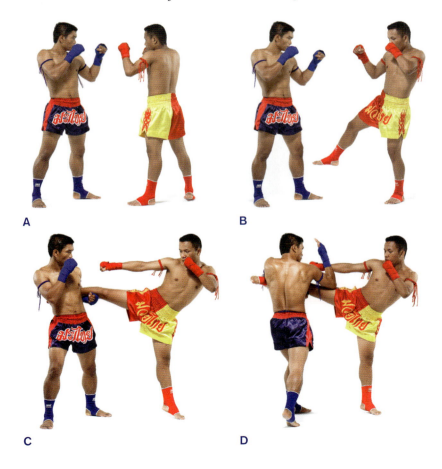

A   B

C   D

Counters against Kicking Techniques

S14: Catch and Kick against the Pivot Leg
■ **Opponent's technique: round kick to the body**

Execution

This counter is carried out once an attack to the pivot leg has been caught. Take a step away from the kick while catching the leg, and hold it firmly below your armpit. Your other arm is held high in front of your face for protection. Next, push down your opponent's lower leg while delivering a kick from the rear to the pivot leg. Due to the turn of the lower leg, your opponent loses control.

If catching the lower leg has been misjudged, there is always a risk that the opponent's technique will hit your ribs, which is the reason why some coaches do not train in it. Other coaches, however, are convinced that the technique is effective, provided the athlete has developed the correct timing in training.

A–D: *Saiyok (left) moves slightly to the outside and catches his opponent's right kick. He promptly turns down the lower leg and follows with a kick from the rear to the pivot leg.*

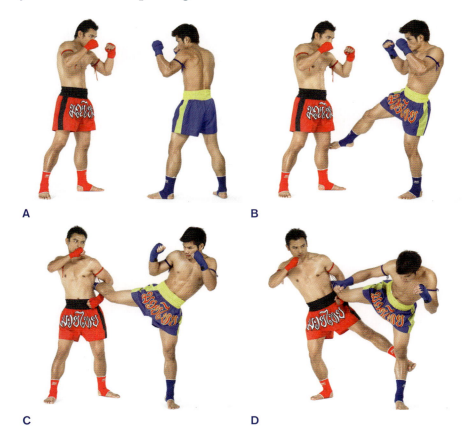

Muay Thai Counter Techniques

A–E: *Taweesak (left) demonstrates the technique against a left kick. Initially he takes a step to the outside left and catches the kick. Than he delivers an effective kick to the pivot leg.*

A

B

C

D

E

S15: Catch and Sweep
◼ **Opponent's technique: round kick to the body**

Execution

In this counter, catch a round kick and floor your opponent with a sweep to the pivot leg. Take a step away from the kick while catching the leg. Pull it up and apply a grip with your other arm to your opponent's head or shoulder. At the same time, push toward the shoulder and carry out a sweep to bring your opponent down. Alternatively, you can carry out a sweep from the rear against the pivot leg.

If you carry out a sweep from the rear, you must push your opponent away from you using your outer arm. If you carry out a sweep from the front, apply a diagonal grip to the other side of the shoulder and pull your opponent in.

A–D: *Nonsai (left) moves slightly to the left away from the kick and catches his opponent's leg. He promptly pulls the leg up and grabs the side of the head with his outer hand. He then floors his opponent by pushing and a sweep from the rear.*

Muay Thai Counter Techniques

S16: Catch and Turn In
■ **Opponent's technique: round kick to the body**

Execution

You can use this technique against a round kick to the body. Take a step away from the kick while catching your opponent's leg. Hold it firmly before you turn it down in a jerk so that your opponent loses control. In the process, you can move your outer foot slightly back. Next, deliver a powerful kick or knee with your rear leg. Be sure that your free hand protects your head.

Alternatively, you can briefly hold the leg before a sudden push to the side.

A–D: *Saiyok (right) moves slightly away from the kick and catches his opponent's leg. He promptly and forcefully turns the lower leg down and follows with a kick from the rear.*

6. Defense against Catch
S17: Straight Punch against a Catch
▮ Opponent's technique: catching a round kick

Execution

If your opponent attempts to catch your round kick, you can stop it with a straight punch with your opposite arm. Lean your body toward your opponent and shift your weight forward for powerful execution. The precondition for the success of this technique is that you do not lean far back with your body when kicking.

The technique is particularly effective if your opponent does not protect the head with the other hand. Even if your opponent does so, he or she must defend against the blow and must interrupt the catching motion.

A–D: *Saiyok (left) carries out a kick to the body. His opponent lowers his arm to catch the kick. Saiyok promptly frees himself with a straight punch from the front.*

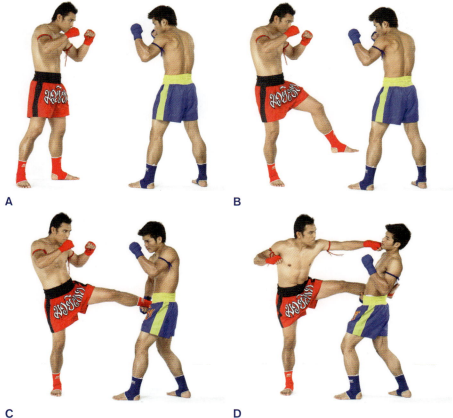

A B

C D

S18: Turn of the Hip and Elbow Hit
Opponent's technique: catching a round kick

Execution

Use this counter for defense if your opponent tries to catch your round kick. Move quickly close to your opponent and stabilize your stand. To this end, fold in your leg, push your hip forward, and turn your knee slightly down. Next, attack the unprotected side of the head with a side elbow or a rotating elbow. Then pull your leg out of your opponent's hold, as your opponent is unable to maintain a grip due to the impact of your elbow. Subsequently, you can use your other arm for an uppercut elbow or a rotating elbow. Be sure to move your leg powerfully and rapidly.

As an option, you can grab your opponent's neck with your front arm and follow with an uppercut elbow with your rear arm.

A–E: *The opponent attempts to catch a round kick to the body. Taweesak (left) folds in the kicking leg, moves close to the opponent, and delivers an elbow technique.*

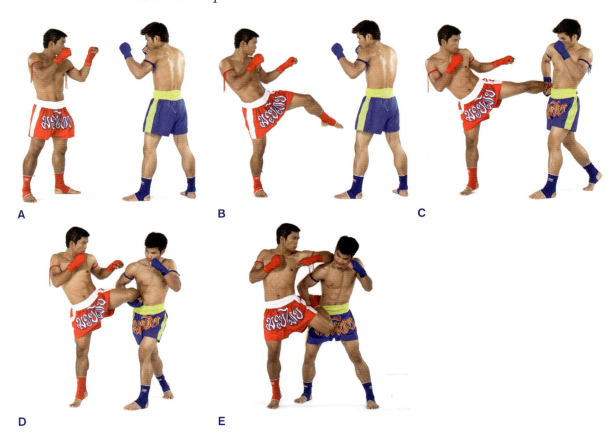

S19: Twisting the Leg Out
■ Opponent's technique: catching a round kick

Execution

If your opponent moves the arm down to catch your kick, twist your lower leg down with force. Pull your leg firmly out of his grip and continue to move it in the direction of the kick. In direct sequence, turn your back toward your opponent while jumping off the floor. Use the momentum generated by the rotation and the jump to carry out a powerful knee kick. As an alternative, you can deliver an elbow technique or a round kick out of the jump.

You can also put your leg on the floor and deliver a reverse elbow without rotation from this position. After a right kick, follow with a right reverse elbow, and after a left kick, a left reverse elbow.

A–F: *The opponent tries to catch the active leg. Taweesak (left) twists his lower leg down with force, thereby releasing his leg from his opponent's grip. He promptly turns counterclockwise and, in the course of his rotation, delivers a jumping knee kick.*

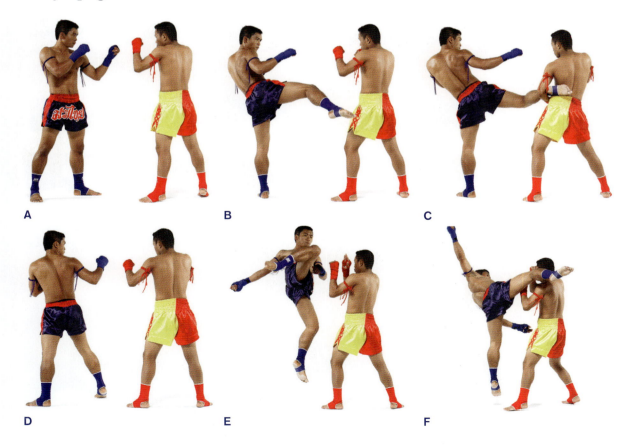

Kem stops his training partner Sitthichai with a push kick.
Bangkok, 2012.

Chapter 6

Counters against Pushing Foot Techniques

1. Introduction

Push kicks are carried out swiftly, and they require prompt reaction as defense. You can forestall your opponent's action by launching your own attack, for which a side step with simultaneous side hook is useful.

You can avoid the kick by taking a step back, leaning back, or retracting your leg. You can also take a step to the outside and deflect the kick to the inside. Your opponent will now be in an unfavorable fight position, enabling you to deliver an effective counter. Advanced athletes can also open up the inner track by deflecting the kick and promptly answering with a kick of their own. A push kick can be blocked with your knee. To this end, deliver the knee on the same side of the body with the inside out. If you succeed in catching the push kick, you can push the leg to the outside, pull it in, or lift it up to throw your opponent back. The subsequent technique depends on the respective counter. You should also train to defend against an opponent's attempts to grab your leg. Hold your balance, and follow promptly with a straight punch.

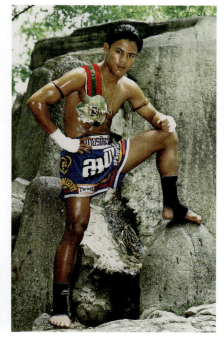

Wiwat Choo-Ubon, fighting name Khunpinit Kiethawan, was born in 1979. His home is Pattalung Province, and his training camp is Kaewsamrit. He has had about 135 professional fights and is a former Lumpinee featherweight champion.

Direct Counter

T1: Step to the Inside with Side Hook
Opponent's technique: front kick, side kick

Avoid and Deflect

T2: Step Back
Opponent's technique: front kick, side kick, back kick

T3: Lean Back
Opponent's technique: push kick to the head or chest

T4: Pull the Leg Back
Opponent's technique: push kick to the front leg

T5: Step to the Outside with Deflection
Opponent's technique: front kick, side kick

T6: Deflecting Sideways to Open the Inside
Opponent's technique: front kick

Counters against Pushing Foot Techniques

Block

T7: Block and Attack
Opponent's technique: front kick to the body or leg

Catch

T8: Catch and Push to the Outside
Opponent's technique: front kick to the body

T9: Catch and Pull In
Opponent's technique: front kick to the body

T10: Catch and Knee Kick
Opponent's technique: front kick to the body

T11: Catch and Push Kick
Opponent's technique: front kick to the body

T12: Catch and Lift
Opponent's technique: front kick to the body or chest

Defense against Catch

T13: Straight Punch against Catch
Opponent's technique: catching a push kick

2. Direct Counter
T1: Step to the Inside with Side Hook
■ Opponent's technique: front kick, side kick

Execution
You can use this direct counter against push kicks if you move very fast. Take a side step away from the attack while delivering a side hook with your outer arm. In the conventional stance, change your stance with a step to the right, and as a southpaw to the left. Be sure that the hook impacts on the return of the foot to the floor, and that you put your weight on it. Subsequently you can follow up with an elbow or knee kick.

A–C: *The opponent attacks with a high push kick. Christoph (left) defends himself by taking a side step and delivering a side hook.*

A B C

Counters against Pushing Foot Techniques

A–D: *Saraya (right) uses a side step with a side hook against a jumping push kick. In the process, he changes his stance. His hook finds his opponent's head if his opponent is moving down or lands on the floor.*

A

B

C

D

3. Avoid and Deflect
T2: Step Back
■ **Opponent's technique: front kick, side kick, back kick**

Execution

In this counter, protect yourself against your opponent's kicking technique by taking a wide step back in a straight line or to the side. In the process, you can deflect the push kick to the side. For defense against a high kick, you can also lean back with your upper body. Follow up with a technique from the rear. To this end, a round kick or a jumping technique is suitable, depending on the distance to your opponent. If your opponent moves far to the front when kicking, you can also counter with a rear straight.

A–D: *The opponent delivers a front kick to the body. Danthai (right) takes a wide step back and follows up with a powerful straight punch, for which he moves forward again.*

A B
C D

Counters against Pushing Foot Techniques

A–F: Taweesak (left) defends himself against a side kick with a wide step back. When missing the target, his opponent falls slightly forward. Taweesak now jumps off the floor and counters with an elbow technique.

Muay Thai Counter Techniques

T3: Lean Back
■ **Opponent's technique: push kick to the head or chest**

Execution

Defend against a push kick to the head by leaning back with your upper body. To this end, step back with your rear foot. Follow up with a powerful technique from the rear, such as a round kick, knee kick, or straight punch. Be sure to maintain your guard with at least one hand held up high and to pull your chin slightly toward your chest for protection of the larynx. Leaning back can also be combined with a step to the rear.

A–E: *The opponent delivers a side kick to the head. Rit (right) leans back with his upper body and follows with a round kick to the head.*

Counters against Pushing Foot Techniques

A–E: *The opponent delivers a front kick to the head. Saiyok (right) leans back with his upper body and follows with a round kick to the body with his rear leg.*

A

B

C

D

E

Muay Thai Counter Techniques

T4: Pull the Leg Back
■ **Opponent's technique: push kick to the front leg**

Execution

This counter is used against an opponent's push kick to the front leg. Pull back the leg that's under attack so that your opponent's kick misses its target. In the process, your upper body will turn along with it, in one swift movement. Follow up with a round kick or a knee kick using the leg that you pulled back previously.

A–D: *The opponent attacks with a push kick to the leg. Danthai (right) pulls back the leg that's under attack and changes his stance before he counters with a round kick.*

A

B

C

D

Counters against Pushing Foot Techniques

T5: Step to the Outside with Deflection
■ **Opponent's technique: front kick, side kick**

Execution

In this counter, move to the outside and deflect the kick to the inside. The deflection can be carried out with the inner or outer hand. Do not hold on to the kicking leg, but push it away in a consistent motion. If your opponent kicks with the left leg, take a step to the right and deflect the kick to the left. The conventional stance requires a change in stance. Against a kick with the right leg, move to the left and deflect the kick to the right. In this case, southpaws must change the stance. Depending on the distance to your opponent, counter with a straight punch, a knee kick, or a kick.

A–E: *The opponent attacks with a left front kick. Christoph (left) deflects the technique to the side while taking a step to the right and changing the stance. He promptly follows with a round kick.*

Muay Thai Counter Techniques

A–E: *The counter against a right front kick. Christoph deflects the technique to the side and follows with a round kick. Alternatively, he can use a knee kick.*

Counters against Pushing Foot Techniques

T6: Deflecting Sideways to Open the Inside

■ **Opponent's technique: front kick**

Execution

Deflect the front kick to the side, thereby opening the inner track. It is important to follow up promptly with a technique; otherwise, your opponent can deliver a punch. Deflect the kick with your opposite hand to the side while taking a step away from the kick. Promptly follow up with a round kick to the head. As an alternative, you can kick with the heel to the chin.

A–D: *Taweesak (left) deflects the front kick to the side and takes a side step. He follows up with a round kick.*

E: *The counter with a side kick.*

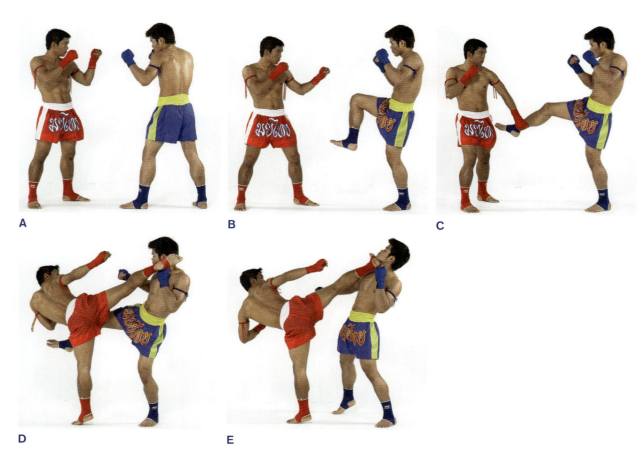

4. Block
T7: Block and Attack
■ **Opponent's technique: front kick to the body or leg**

Execution

In this counter, block a front kick with the knee away to the side. Push the kick from the inside out with the knee on the same side of the body, as if initially delivering the knee kick to the front, and then move it sideways in the course of the move. Rest the pushing leg on the floor behind you, and follow up with an attacking technique such as a round kick. Watch your balance and hold your arms up high for protection.

A–D: *Kem (left) blocks a front kick to the left. He then rests his pushing leg on the floor behind him and follows with a round kick from this position.*

5. Catch
T8: Catch and Push to the Outside
■ **Opponent's technique:** front kick to the body

Execution

Defend against the front kick by taking a step back. At the same time, catch the kick with your front hand, applying a firm grip around the Achilles tendon. With your other hand, you can grab from above to stabilize your position. Briefly hold the leg before you push it out. Follow up with a round kick from the rear.

A–D: *The opponent attacks with a front kick to the body. Saiyok (right) takes a step back and catches the kicking leg. He briefly holds on to it before pushing it to the side. He now follows with a round kick.*

A

B

C

D

T9: Catch and Pull In
■ **Opponent's technique: front kick to the body**

Execution

In this counter, catch the leg and pull it in. To this end, first take a step back and catch the front kick. Apply the grip with the front hand from below around the Achilles tendon, and put the other hand on the foot. Next, pull your opponent toward you in a jerk, so that your opponent falls forward, and launch your attack with an uppercut elbow from the rear. A knee kick is a possible alternative.

A–D: *The opponent attacks with a front kick. Kem (left) takes a step back and catches the leg. He then pulls it in and follows up with an uppercut elbow.*

A

B

C

D

Counters against Pushing Foot Techniques

T10: Catch and Knee Kick
Opponent's technique: front kick to the body

Execution

In this counter, catch the forward kick in a shovel-like move by grabbing the leg from below. At the same time, you can take a small step back. It is important to hold the leg firmly around the Achilles tendon. Your other arm is initially held in front of your face, and subsequently moved promptly from the inside to your opponent's neck. The diagonal grip protects you against punching techniques. Then pull your opponent toward you and carry out a powerful knee kick.

A–D: *The opponent attacks with a front kick to the body. Taweesak (left) deflects the leg slightly to the side and grabs it in the process. He then pulls his opponent in and delivers a knee kick.*

A B C D

T11: Catch and Push Kick
◼ Opponent's technique: front kick to the body

Execution

In this counter, catch the push kick and follow up with your own kick. Initially, take a step back, and catch your opponent's kick in the process. Grab with your front hand from below, and put your other hand on the foot. Pull your opponent toward you while delivering a powerful front kick with your rear leg.

A–D: *The opponent attacks with a front kick. Nonsai (left) catches the kick, pulls his opponent toward him, and floors him with a front kick.*

A

B

C

D

Counters against Pushing Foot Techniques

T12: **Catch and Lift**
Opponent's technique: front kick to the body or chest

Execution

This counter succeeds well if your opponent kicks chest-high. Defend by taking a step back and catching the kicking leg. Grab firmly from below around the Achilles tendon, and put your other hand on the foot. Then lift the leg so that your opponent is put off-balance and falls down. Follow up with a round or knee kick carried out from the rear side of your body.

A–D: *The opponent attacks with a front kick. Nonsai (left) takes a step back and catches the kicking leg. He then lifts the leg and follows up with a round kick.*

A

B

C

D

6. Defense against Catch
T13: Straight Punch against Catch
■ Opponent's technique: catching a push kick

Execution

Use this counter if your opponent tries to catch your front kick. Once your opponent moves his or her arm down to apply the grip, deliver a straight punch with your opposite arm. Move your weight forward to succeed in powerful delivery. A precondition for success is to keep your body almost upright during the kick.

A–D: *Taweesak (left) delivers a push kick to the body. His opponent moves his front arm down to catch the kick. Taweesak defends himself with a straight punch.*

A

B

C

D

A straight knee kick from Nonsai.
Bangkok, 2012.

Chapter 7

Counters against Knee Techniques from a Distance

1. Introduction

Powerful knee techniques from a distance are very dangerous and can often result in a knockout. Practice a number of action patterns for as long as it takes to use them instinctively. That will enable you to stand up against even the best Thai fighters. Always be sure to hold your guard up high, as your opponent can follow up with an elbow.

As a direct counter against knee kicks, you can use a front straight punch, a kick to the pivot leg, an elbow to the thigh, or a step to the inside in combination with a side hook. You can avoid a knee kick by taking a large step back. You can also take a step to the outside or inside, and deflect the knee kick in the course of the move. If you plan to block a knee kick, it is best to push with the knee on the same side of the body. It is important to aim for the inside of the thigh. You can also catch a knee kick and follow up with an effective counterattack. After the catch, you must promptly insure that your opponent is put off-balance by lifting the leg slightly. Subsequently, it is best to follow up with a knee kick or a sweep.

Adisak Duangyai, fighting name Nongbee Kietyongyuth, was born in 1981. His home is Nakhon Srithamarat Province. He has had about 134 professional fights and was Rajadamnern champion and Lumpinee featherweight champion.

Muay Thai Counter Techniques

DIRECT COUNTER

K1: Front Straight Punch
Opponent's technique: all knee kicks

K2: Push Kick
Opponent's technique: all knee kicks

K3: Elbow to the Thigh
Opponent's technique: straight knee kick, lateral knee kick

K4: Step to the Inside with a Side Hook
Opponent's technique: all knee kicks

AVOID AND DEFLECT

K5: Step Back
Opponent's technique: all knee kicks

K6: Step to the Outside with Deflection
Opponent's technique: straight knee kick

K7: Side Step and Round Kick
Opponent's technique: jumping knee kick

BLOCK

K8: Knee Block to the Inside of the Thigh
Opponent's technique: straight knee kick, lateral knee kick

K9: Step to the Inside and Block
Opponent's technique: straight knee kick, lateral knee kick

CATCH

K10: Catch and Knee Kick
Opponent's technique: straight knee kick, lateral knee kick

K11: Catch and Sweep
Opponent's technique: straight knee kick, lateral knee kick

2. Direct Counter
K1: Front Straight Punch
■ Opponent's technique: all knee kicks

Execution

In this counter, defend with a front straight punch against a knee kick. To this end, take a step forward. It is important that you stretch your arm and shift your weight to the front. Due to the punch, your opponent is put off-balance, and the kicking motion will be stopped. Subsequently, depending on the distance to your opponent, deliver additional attacking techniques such as a knee kick with your rear leg.

In training, practice the technique as a slight push with the palm of your hand to your opponent's ribcage. The technique should be carried out in such a way that your partner is put slightly off-balance.

A–D: *The opponent attacks with a straight knee kick. Christoph (left) defends himself with a front straight punch.*

Muay Thai Counter Techniques

K2: Push Kick

■ Opponent's technique: all knee kicks

Execution

A push kick can be used as defense against all possible knee kicks from a distance. It is best to deliver the kick with your front foot to the pivot leg slightly above the knee. An option is to deliver the kick to the stomach. Once you have stopped your opponent with the kick, return your leg to the floor in front of you, and follow up with a round kick from the rear.

A–D: *The opponent attacks with a knee kick. Khunsap (right) stops the attack with a push kick from the front. He returns his leg to the floor in front on him and follows with a high kick.*

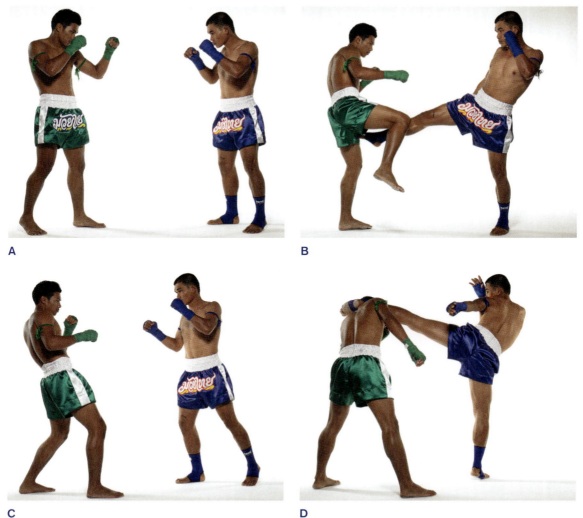

A

B

C

D

Counters against Knee Techniques from a Distance

K3: Elbow to the Thigh
■ Opponent's technique: straight knee kick, lateral knee kick

Execution

Protect yourself against your opponent's knee kick by hitting the elbow on the same side of the body to the center of the thigh. If you hit with your rear elbow, your rear leg moves forward. Then rotate swiftly on your front leg. From a conventional stance, rotate clockwise; as a southpaw, counterclockwise. Use the momentum gained by the rotation to deliver your rear elbow laterally to the jaw or from below to the chin. It is important that you deliver the first hit directly out of the defensive stance and that you don't lower your arm, as your opponent could follow with an elbow.

A–E: *Taweesak (left) uses an elbow hit against a knee kick. He steps forward with his right leg, turns on this leg, and follows with a spinning elbow.*

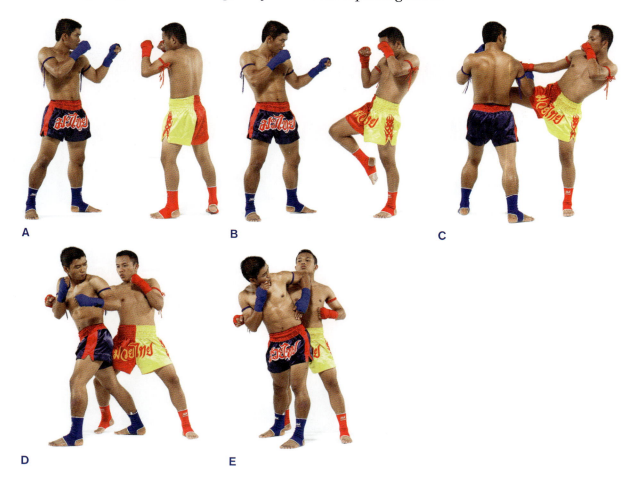

A   B   C

D   E

Muay Thai Counter Techniques

K4: Step to the Inside with a Side Hook
■ Opponent's technique: all knee kicks

Execution

In this counter, dodge to the inside while delivering a side hook from the outside. Take a step forward with your outer foot. From a conventional stance, the stance changes with a step to the right; southpaws, with a step to the left. Be sure that the hook impacts when your foot returns to the floor, and that you put your weight behind it. You can promptly follow with a rotating elbow of the hitting arm.

To avoid injury in your training, only push your partner's chest with the palm of your hand.

A–D: *The opponent attacks with a knee kick from a distance. Christoph (left) defends himself by taking a step to the right with his right leg and changes his stance before he delivers a simultaneous side hook.*

A

B

C

D

Counters against Knee Techniques from a Distance

3. Avoid and Deflect
K5: Step Back

■ **Opponent's technique: all knee kicks**

Execution

Defend against a knee kick by taking a wide step back. The step can be in a diagonal or straight line to the rear. Having missed the target, your opponent will be in an unfavorable position so that you can carry out an effective round kick to the head. Advanced athletes deliver the follow-up technique in a jump.

As an alternative, you can use a powerful straight punch or an elbow, for which you have to take a step forward.

A–D: *The opponent attacks with a straight knee kick. Taweesak (left) defends himself by stepping back and follows with a jumping round kick.*

A

B

C

D

K6: Step to the Outside with Deflection
■ Opponent's technique: straight knee kick

Execution

In this counter, defend yourself against a straight knee kick by taking a step to the outside while deflecting the kick to the inside. From a conventional stance, the stance must be changed by taking a step to the right; southpaws change stance by stepping to the left. Follow up with an elbow that has your weight behind it. Pay particular attention to protecting your head.

The deflection and follow-up technique can be carried out by the inner or outer side of the body. Choose instinctively which option is best suited for your fight style.

A–D: *The opponent attacks with a knee kick from a distance. Armin (left) takes a step forward to the left and deflects the kick to the right. He then follows up with a rotating elbow.*

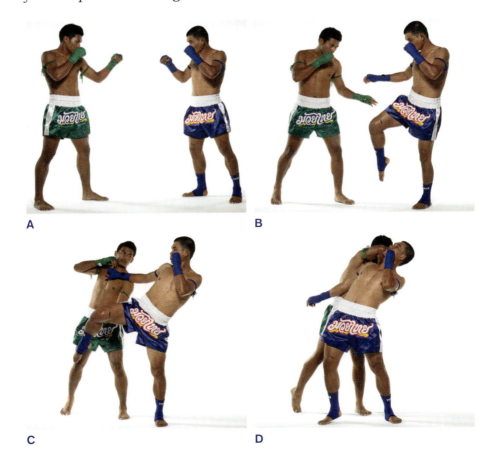

A B

C D

Counters against Knee Techniques from a Distance

K7: Side Step and Round Kick
▪ Opponent's technique: jumping knee kick

Execution

Defend yourself against a flying knee kick by taking a quick side step. If your opponent delivers a right knee kick, move to the right. If your opponent attacks with the left knee, however, take a step to the left. You will now face your opponent sideways and counter with a round kick to the back. Be sure to carry out the step and counter kick in direct sequence.

A–D: *The opponent starts with a jumping knee kick. Rit (left) guards himself by taking a step to the right. He promptly counters with a round kick to the back. He could also kick with his inner leg, but this entails the risk of injury due to his opponent's pointed knee.*

A
B
C
D

4. Block

K8: Knee Block to the Inside of the Thigh

■ **Opponent's technique: straight knee kick, lateral knee kick**

Execution

In this counter, block to the inside of the thigh. To this end, first move your knee forward before you turn it to hit the center of the thigh. Subsequently, you can follow up with a rotating elbow from the same side. Pay attention to keeping your guard up high, as your opponent can follow with an elbow technique.

A–D: *The opponent attacks with a straight knee kick. Danthai (right) defends himself by kicking to the inside of the thigh.*

E: *Block of a knee kick with the left leg.*

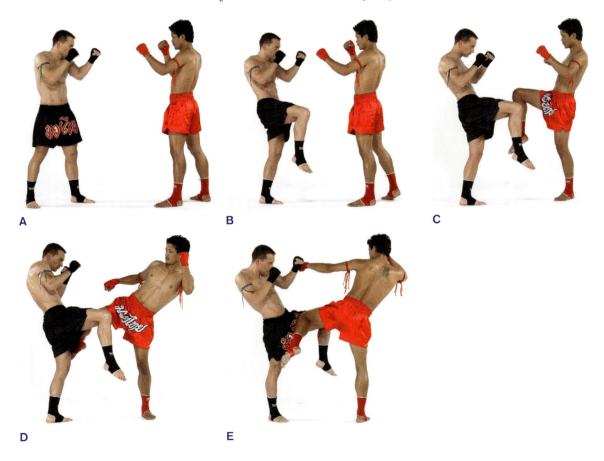

Counters against Knee Techniques from a Distance

K9: Step to the Inside and Block
■ **Opponent's technique: straight knee kick, lateral knee kick**

Execution

Deflect your opponent's knee kick with your opposite arm to the outside while taking a step away from the knee kick. The block is carried out in such a manner that you hit the lower arm down to the outside, thus stretching the arm. From a conventional stance, the stance has to be changed with the step to the right; southpaws with the step to the left. In direct sequence, deliver a rotating elbow with the outer arm.

The technique is most suitable for advanced athletes, as any misjudgment entails the risk of your opponent's following up with an elbow.

A–D: *The opponent attacks with a right knee kick. Taweesak (left) takes a step to the right and blocks the knee kick to the outside. He promptly follows up with a rotating elbow.*

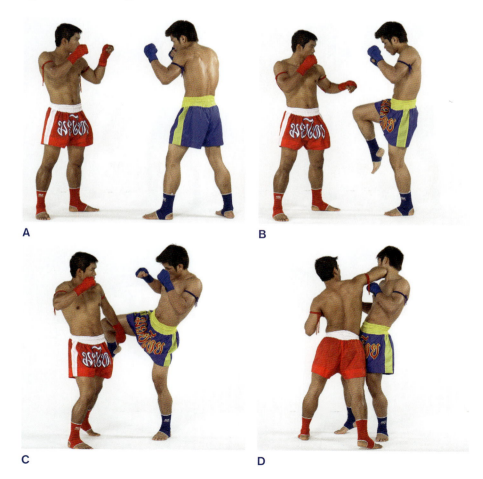

A B

C D

5. Catch

K10: Catch and Knee Kick

■ Opponent's technique: straight knee kick, lateral knee kick

Execution

In this counter, defend yourself by taking a step away from the knee kick while catching it. Grab your opponent's leg from below with your inner hand. Promptly lift the leg so that your opponent is put off-balance and is unable to deliver an elbow. Next attack your opponent with your other arm, pull him or her toward you, and deliver a knee kick. Options are a punch or elbow technique.

A–D: *The opponent attacks with a knee kick from a distance. Kem (left) defends himself by taking a step to the right while catching the leg. He swiftly lifts the leg, grabs his opponent, and follows with a knee kick.*

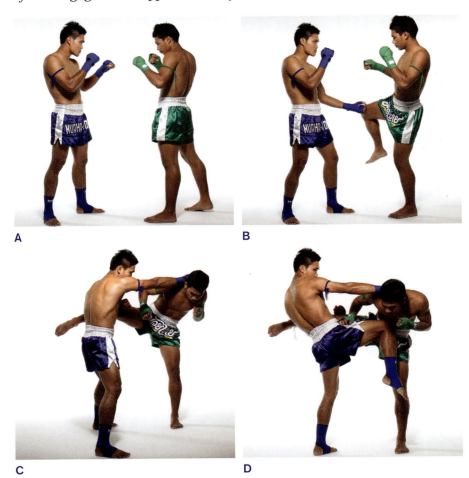

A B

C D

Counters against Knee Techniques from a Distance

K11: Catch and Sweep

■ Opponent's technique: straight knee kick, lateral knee kick

Execution

Defend yourself against a knee kick by taking a step away from the kick. Catch the leg, and lift it up high enough for your opponent to be put off-balance. Next push the other arm diagonally to the shoulder, and floor your opponent with a sweep from the front.

As an alternative, you can carry out the sweep against the pivot leg from the rear using your inner leg.

A–E: *Saiyok (right) takes a step to the right while catching his opponent's kicking leg. He promptly pushes it up and grabs his opponent's shoulder. He now follows up with a sweep to the inside of the leg.*

Saiyok and Armin in clinch training.
Bangkok, 2012.

Chapter 8

Counters against Clinch Techniques

1. Introduction

In a clinch situation, you must master techniques that enable you to control your opponent. In addition, learn the defenses against your opponent's knee kicks and grip techniques.

If you succeed in applying a stable grip to achieve an advantageous clinch position, you can control your opponent by pulling him or her along, throwing, pushing, and shoving away. If your opponent attacks in a clinch with a knee kick, you can defend yourself by blocking the attack, attacking the pivot leg, or by pushing your opponent to the floor. If your opponent has applied a stable grip in a clinch, you can escape by pushing the arm up or down. You can also free yourself with a turn of your body and by pushing your opponent away to the front. If your opponent tries to move inside your grip by grabbing from below, however, block the arm and follow with an elbow or a knee technique.

Control of the Opponent

C1: Pull Along to the Side
Opponent's position: unstable grip with arms outside

C2: Pull Along to the Rear
Opponent's position: unstable grip with arms outside

C3: Push Away
Opponent's position: unstable grip

C4: Pressure to the Ribs and Throw
Opponent's position: unstable grip with arms up

C5: Pressure to the Ribs and Knee Kick
Opponent's position: unstable grip with arms up

C6: Push to the Floor and Throw
Opponent's position: unstable grip with arms up

C7: Cover the Face and Knee Kicks
Opponent's position: wide body clearance

C8: Throw to the Side
Opponent's position: unstable stance

Counter against Knee Techniques

C9: Turn of the Hip and Knee Kick
Opponent's technique: lateral knee kick

C10: Dodge and Push Down to the Floor
Opponent's technique: all knee kicks

C11: Pull Along in the Direction of the Knee Kick
Opponent's technique: lateral knee kick

C12: Throw in the Direction of the Knee Kick
Opponent's technique: lateral knee kick

C13: Knee Block to the Inside of the Thigh
Opponent's technique: all knee kicks

C14: Sweep
Opponent's technique: all knee techniques

C15: Step Back and Push Down
Opponent's technique: knee kick from the front

Opening a Clinch Grip

C16: Pressure on the Arm and Elbow
Opponent's technique: inner grip

C17: Push the Arm Up and Elbow
Opponent's technique: inner grip

C18: Release by Body Turn and Elbow from Above
Opponent's technique: firm grip around the chest or ribs

C19: Release by Body Turn and Grip from Above
Opponent's technique: firm grip around chest, ribs, or neck

C20: Push Away to the Front and Knee Kick
Opponent's technique: inner grip

C21: Counter Tension and Twisting Out
Opponent's technique: pushing the head down

Counter against Grip Techniques

C22: Block and Rotating Elbow
Opponent's technique: grip from below

C23: Grab the Upper Arm and Throw
Opponent's technique: grip from below

2. Control of the Opponent
C1: Pull Along to the Side

■ Opponent's position: unstable grip with arms outside

Execution

You can use this counter in a clinch once you have applied a stable grip around the neck. Move one foot forward to the outside, and follow with the other foot while pulling your opponent along. Follow up with a knee kick using your inner leg. The technique will also succeed if you hold your opponent's upper arm with one hand and the neck with the other.

A–D: *Christoph (left) has applied a firm grip inside around his opponent's neck. He moves his right leg to the outside, follows with his left, and pulls his opponent along. He then continues with a knee kick to the head.*

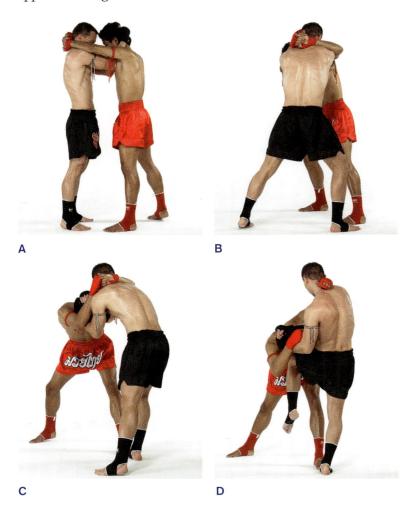

A B

C D

C2: Pull Along to the Rear

■ **Opponent's position: unstable grip with arms outside**

Execution

In this counter, control your opponent with a stable grip around his neck. Move back with one leg while forcefully pulling down your opponent's head. Promptly deliver a knee kick to the head or body with your retracted leg.

A–C: *Christoph (left) controls his opponent with a firm grip inside around the neck. He steps back with one leg while pulling down his opponent's head. He delivers a prompt knee kick to the body.*

A

B

C

A–C: *Danthai (right) demonstrates the technique to the head. He pulls his left leg back while pushing his opponent down in a jerk and follows with a kick to the face.*

A

B

C

Counters against Clinch Techniques

C3: Push Away
Opponent's position: unstable grip

Execution

In this counter, apply an inner grip around the neck, and push your opponent away to the front. Carry out the push with your lower arms in a jerk while slightly moving forward with one leg. Follow up with a knee kick with your rear leg. In the process, you can jump slightly off the floor.

A–D: *Kem (left) has applied a stable inner grip. He pushes his opponent away with his lower arms and follows up with a right knee kick.*

A

B

C

D

C4: Pressure to the Ribs and Throw

■ Opponent's position: unstable grip with arms up

Execution

If your opponent tries to apply a grip to your head, react with a powerful grip high around the ribs. Stabilize the position by putting your hands on top of each other behind your opponent's back. As an alternative, you can grab your own elbows and stabilize your position that way. A stable stance is important, and to that end you can slightly bend your legs. Push hard against the ribs, causing your opponent to have difficulty breathing. Next move forward with one foot, and throw your opponent across your knee.

A–D: *Armin (right) grabs his opponent around the lower ribs. He steps forward with his left leg and throws his opponent aside.*

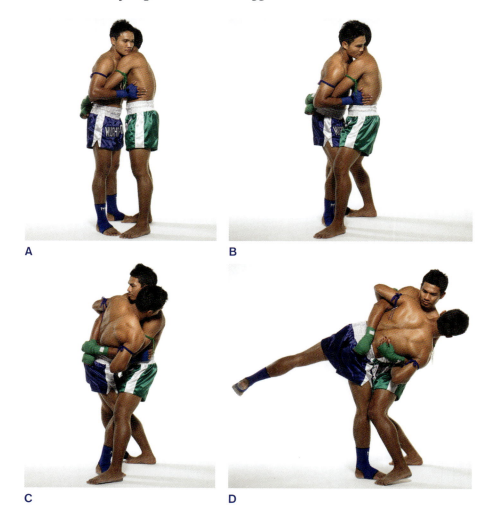

A

B

C

D

C5: Pressure to the Ribs and Knee Kick
■ Opponent's position: unstable grip with arms up

Execution

In this counter, defend yourself against a grip to the neck by firmly grabbing your opponent around the ribs. Put your hands above each other at rib level, or grab your own elbow to stabilize your position. Initially, push hard against the ribs, then retract one leg and deliver your knee to the stomach or thigh. Additionally, you can push with your chin on your opponent's shoulder blade, thereby causing pain.

A–D: *Taweesak (left) grabs firmly around his opponent's ribs and squeezes hard. He then pulls his right leg back and follows up with a knee kick to the stomach.*

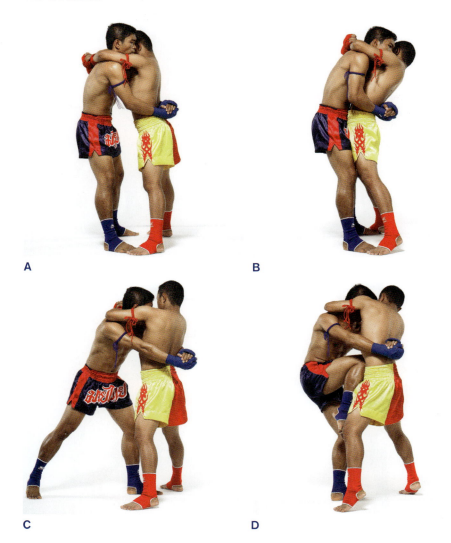

A B

C D

C6: Push to the Floor and Throw
■ Opponent's position: unstable grip with arms up

Execution

You can use this counter after a grip around your ribs. Fix your position by grabbing your wrist or elbow, and push hard against the ribs so that your opponent has difficulty breathing. Bend your knees slightly to achieve a stable stance. Subsequently, lift your opponent before you push him or her back to the floor, and finally, throw your opponent sideways.

A–D: *Taweesak (left) applies a firm grip around the ribs and bends his knees slightly. Having lifted his opponent, he pushes him back to the floor and throws him sideways.*

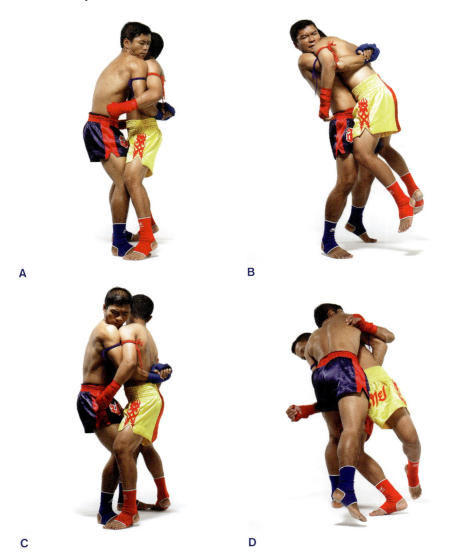

C7: **Cover the Face and Knee Kicks**
■ **Opponent's position: wide body clearance**

Execution

If your opponent attempts to apply a grip, or the grip is unstable, place the palm of your hand on your opponent's face and your other hand on top of it. Stretch your arms and push your opponent's head backward. Keep your opponent at a distance, and attack with knee kicks.

The technique is best used if your opponent concentrates on carrying out a technique. Even though your opponent will try to hit your hands away, you will succeed in delivering a knee kick beforehand, and you can swiftly end the fight with your follow-up techniques.

A–D: *The opponent attempts to apply the inner clinch grip. Taweesak (left) covers his opponent's face with his hands and pushes his head away. He then follows up with knee techniques.*

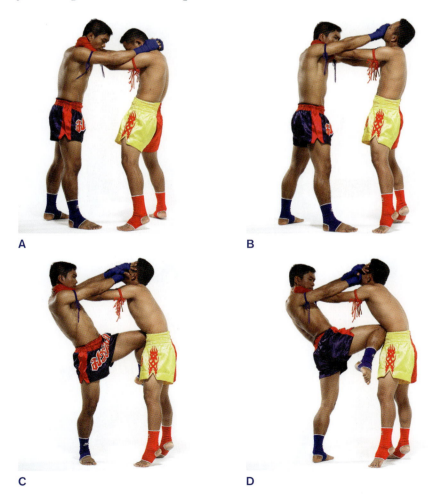

Muay Thai Counter Techniques

C8: Throw to the Side
■ Opponent's position: unstable stance

Execution

In this counter, throw your opponent when in a clinch. Initially, take a stable stance and grab with one hand around your opponent's neck. Put your other hand under the armpit, or fix the upper arm. Next pull your opponent's head in a jerk, and at the same time, push against the armpit or upper arm to throw the opponent sideways. It is important to carry out the move in a jerk and to turn your body along with the move.

A–D: *Taweesak (left) has a stable stance. One hand is on the neck and the other on the upper arm. He throws his opponent in a jerk to the left and turns along with the move.*

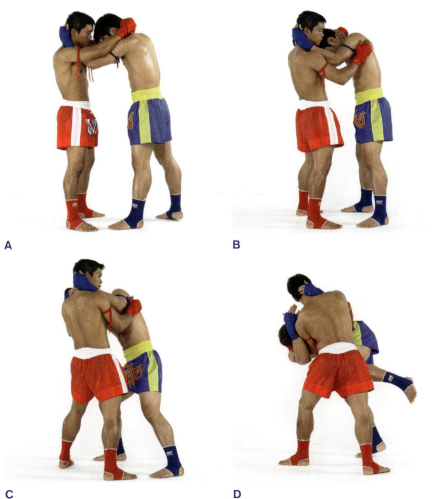

A

B

C

D

Counters against Clinch Techniques

3. Counter against Knee Techniques

C9: Turn of the Hip and Knee Kick

■ Opponent's technique: lateral knee kick

Execution

Use this counter against a knee kick from the side. Defend yourself by turning your hip in and moving toward your opponent. With this technique you will be struck by the thigh instead of the knee, which will generate only slight impact. Against a knee kick with the left, turn to the left and move forward with the right side of your hip. Against a right knee kick, react the other way round. Return your leg on the same side of the body to the floor and follow up with a knee kick.

As a variant, you can hit the hip on the inside of the thigh, which will also generate some impact.

A–D: *The opponent delivers a lateral knee kick with the left. Kem (right) defends himself by turning his body to the left. He then retracts his right leg and follows up with a powerful knee kick.*

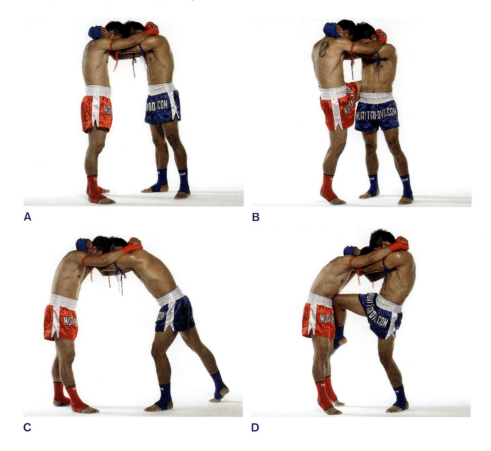

A B

C D

Muay Thai Counter Techniques

C10: Dodge and Push Down to the Floor
■ **Opponent's technique: all knee kicks**

Execution

In this counter, push your opponent down to the floor opposite to the direction of the kick. For defense against the knee kick, initially move your outer foot slightly to the outside. Then follow with your other foot and push your opponent with a jerk opposite to the direction of the kick. Subsequently, follow up with a knee kick with your inner leg.

A–D: *The opponent (left) attacks with a right knee kick. For your defense, initially move your right foot slightly to the right and follow with your left foot. Your opponent will be pushed down to the floor on the left, followed up by a left knee kick.*

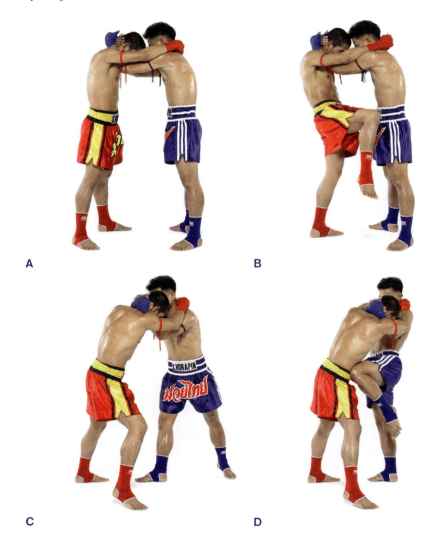

A   B

C   D

C11: Pull Along in the Direction of the Knee Kick

■ **Opponent's technique: lateral knee kick**

Execution

In this counter, pull your opponent along in the direction of the kick and deliver a knee kick. Once your opponent starts with the kicking technique, step back with your outer leg and pull your opponent along. To this end, jerk your opponent with your lower arms on the neck. It is important to move your inner leg far back. Follow up with a knee kick carried out with your retracted leg.

This counter is a good defensive move, but learning the correct timing requires extensive training.

A–D: *The opponent carries out a lateral knee kick in a clinch. Danthai (right) defends himself by hurling his opponent to the right while retracting his right leg. He then follows up with a knee kick to the head.*

A

B

C

D

Muay Thai Counter Techniques

C12: Throw in the Direction of the Knee Kick

■ **Opponent's technique: lateral knee kick**

Execution

In this counter, throw your opponent in the direction of the knee kick. Either put both lower arms firmly around the neck or one hand below the armpit. As soon as your opponent retracts the leg to deliver the knee kick, carry out the throw with a jerk. Turn your body sideways along with the throw, and throw with power.

You will be particularly successful with this technique if your opponent carries out several knee kicks in sequence, as often seen in Thai arenas. Fighters defend themselves, for example, by turning in the hip. In that way, the opponent gets tired and can no longer clinch and kick as hard, making it easier to throw.

A–D: *The opponent retracts his leg and delivers a straight knee kick. Taweesak (left) detects the technique at an early stage and throws his opponent to the left, in the direction of the kick.*

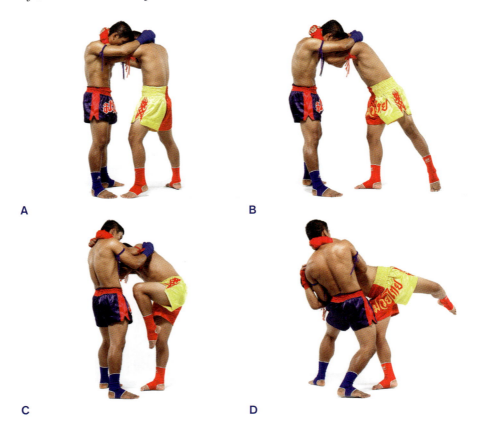

C13: Knee Block to the Inside of the Thigh

■ **Opponent's technique: all knee kicks**

Execution

In this counter, attack the kicking leg with a knee block. Kick with your knee on the same side of the body from inside to the center of the thigh. To this end, first move your knee slightly forward and turn it toward the target. Move your leg to the rear and follow up with a knee kick from there.

Alternatively, you can block a knee kick from the front by hitting the thigh with a straight kick with your opposite knee. You can also deliver a half shin, half knee kick from the front against the thigh to prevent knee kicks. These techniques must be carried out very quickly, as your opponent will otherwise be too far along in the kicking movement.

A–E: *Kem (left) defends himself with a block to the inside of the thigh. He then pulls his leg back and follows up with a knee kick.*

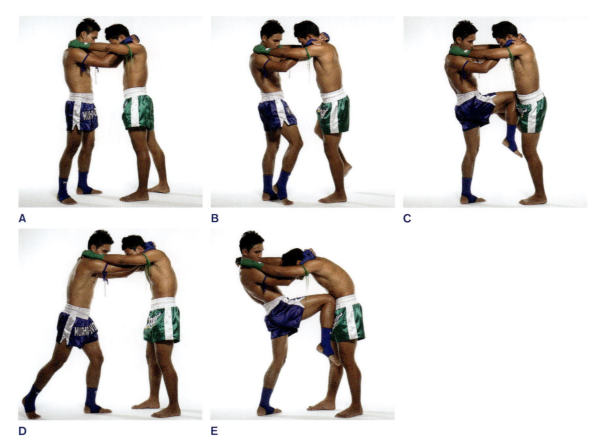

C14: Sweep

Opponent's technique: all knee techniques

Execution

You can use a sweep as a defense against all knee kicks in a clinch. Lean back with your body in the other direction, and pull your opponent along. Hit the lower part of the pivot leg from behind with the lower base of your shin.

Current Muay Thai regulations require that you carry out the counter with your shin and not with the inside of your foot.

A–D: *Armin (right) defends himself against a knee kick with a left sweep. He leans his body to the left and pulls his opponent along.*

A

B

C

D

C15: Step Back and Push Down
Opponent's technique: knee kick from the front

Execution

You can use this counter if your opponent steps back with one foot in order to deliver a powerful knee kick. Defend by pulling your opposite leg back while pushing your opponent's head down. Follow up with a knee kick with your rear leg to the body or head. Pay attention to your timing and push down with a jerk.

A–D: *The opponent retracts his leg to deliver a straight knee kick. Armin (right) retracts his opposite leg and pulls his opponent down. He promptly follows with a knee kick from the rear.*

A

B

C

D

4. Opening a Clinch Grip
C16: Pressure on the Arm and Elbow
■ **Opponent's technique: inner grip**

Execution

Use this counter if your opponent has put his or her lower arms inside around your neck, thereby taking on an advantageous clinch position. Initially put one hand on the center of the arm. Take a step back, shift your weight, and at the same time force the arm down. Follow up with a rotating elbow while moving ahead again. The step to the rear is important as it helps to get out of the grip.

A–D: *The opponent has applied an inner grip. Armin (left) frees himself by jerking his opponent's arm down in combination with a step back. He promptly follows with a rotating elbow to the now unprotected side of the head.*

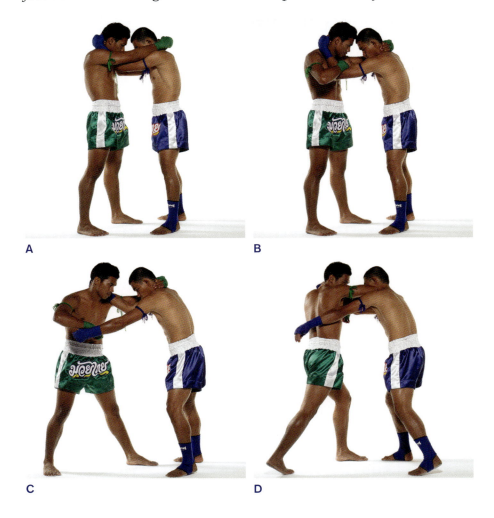

Counters against Clinch Techniques

C17: Push the Arm Up and Elbow
■ Opponent's technique: inner grip

Execution

Your opponent has put his or her lower arms around your neck and is in an advantageous position. Release yourself from the grip by swiftly and energetically pushing your opponent's arm up. To this end, you must grab the elbow joint or the upper arm. At the end of the movement, the head will be unprotected, allowing you to deliver a rotating elbow with the same arm. Shift your weight forward.

A–D: *The opponent has applied an inner grip. Saiyok (left) pushes his opponent's lower arm up and follows promptly with a rotating elbow to the now unprotected side of the head.*

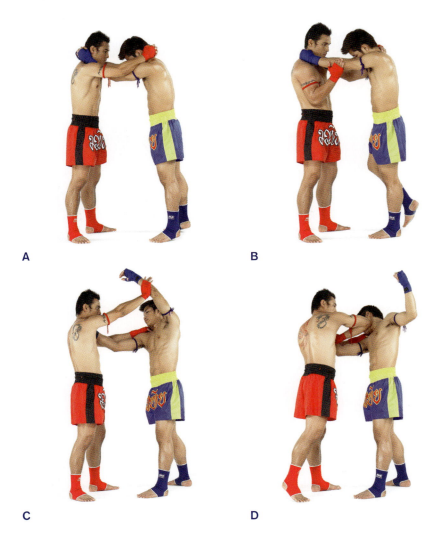

A B

C D

C18: Release by Body Turn and Elbow from Above

■ **Opponent's technique: firm grip around the chest or ribs**

Execution

In a clinch, your opponent has applied a firm grip around the chest or ribs and pulls you powerfully toward him or her. To free yourself from this position, turn laterally toward your opponent while stretching your body and the inner arm up. This will give you air to breathe and some freedom of movement so that you can now deliver a powerful elbow from above to the neck or shoulder blade. Subsequently, use your lower arm to push your opponent away from the neck, and follow up with a knee kick.

A–E: *The opponent has applied a firm grip in a low position. Christoph (left) loosens the grip by turning to the left and stretching the inner arm up. He continues by hitting his elbow from above, and pushes his opponent away. He follows with a straight knee kick.*

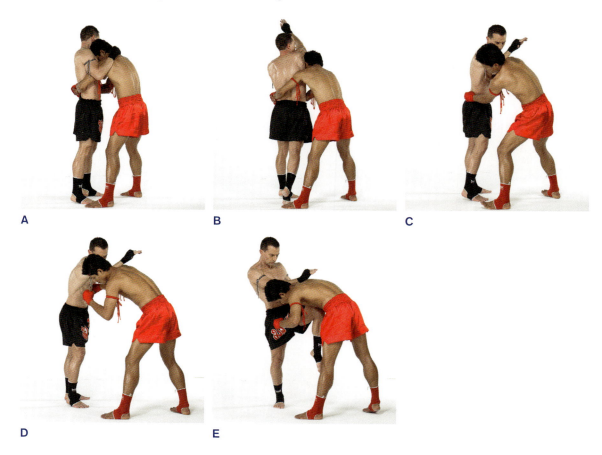

Counters against Clinch Techniques

C19: Release by Body Turn and Grip from Above

■ **Opponent's technique: firm grip around the chest, ribs, or neck**

Execution

Use this counter in a clinch if your opponent pushes against your chest, ribs, or neck. Release yourself by turning sideways. Raise your inner arm in the process, and from above, put it around your opponent's neck. Then pull your inner leg back, and pull your opponent along. Next follow with a powerful knee kick to the body or head.

A–D: *The opponent has applied a firm grip. Armin (left) turns to the left and grabs with his right arm from above. He retracts his right leg and pulls his opponent along. He then follows with a knee kick.*

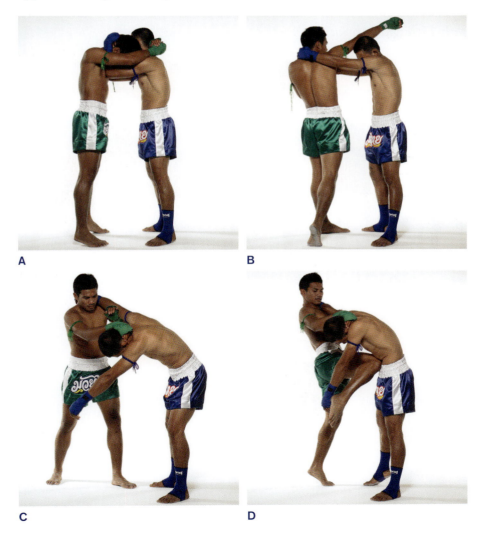

C20: Push Away to the Front and Knee Kick

■ Opponent's technique: inner grip

Execution

If your opponent attempts to apply an inner grip, or the inner grip is not yet firm, you can push your opponent away. From below, put one palm to the chin and the other hand on top of it. Stretch both arms, and push your opponent's chin to the rear. Follow up with a kick or a knee kick from the rear.

Practice the technique in training with only a little power as it entails the danger of hurting your partner by overstretching the head.

A–E: *The opponent attempts to apply a firm inner clinch grip. Danthai (right) defends himself by pushing his opponent's head to the rear. He then follows with a straight knee kick.*

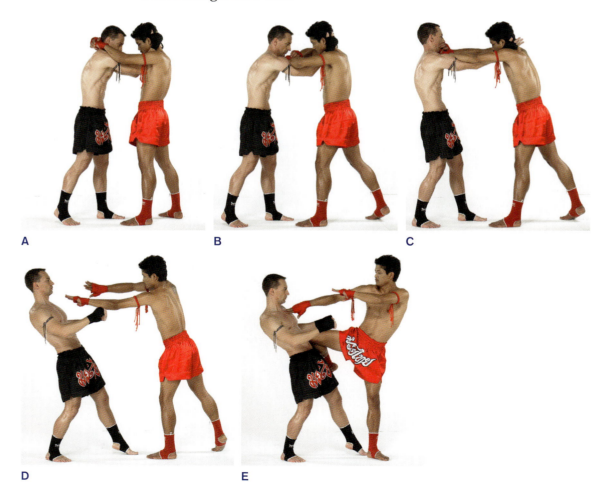

Counters against Clinch Techniques

C21: Counter Tension and Twisting Out
■ **Opponent's technique: pushing the head down**

Execution

Your opponent tries to grab your neck from the inside. Raise your shoulders and arms so that your opponent will not be able to apply a firm grip. At the same time, tense your head against your opponent's hands. In direct sequence, put your left hand on the left shoulder and your right hand next to it on the upper arm. Simultaneously move your left leg to the outside in front of you. Next thrust your head out and twist yourself sideways and clockwise on your left leg out of the grip. Use the momentum gained from the rotation to deliver an elbow technique. During this technique, you can step forward with your rear leg, but this is not absolutely necessary.

You can also put your right hand on your opponent's shoulder and move your right leg forward. If so, you must rotate counterclockwise.

A–D: *The opponent tries to push down Taweesak's head. Taweesak (left) tenses his head against his opponent's grip, puts his hands on the shoulder and upper arm, and moves his left leg forward in the process. He then thrusts his head out, turns clockwise out of the grip, and follows with an elbow technique.*

A

B

C

D

Muay Thai Counter Techniques

5. Counter against Grip Techniques
C22: Block and Rotating Elbow
■ **Opponent's technique: grip from below**

Execution

In this scenario, you have applied the inner grip around your opponent's neck, and your opponent tries to grab from below to move into the inner position. For your defense, turn your elbow to the inside and block the arm down. Step back a little. Follow up with a rotating elbow, and move forward again. Be sure to carry out the block and elbow technique in direct sequence.

In training, push your opponent's arm down with power, but only feint the subsequent elbow technique in order not to hurt your partner.

A–D: *The opponent tries to grab from below. Christoph (left) defends his position by blocking the attack and countering with a rotating elbow.*

A

B

C

D

Counters against Clinch Techniques

C23: Grab the Upper Arm and Throw
▪ **Opponent's technique: grip from below**

Execution

Use this counter if your opponent changes grip position. Hold your opponent's upper arm with a firm grip. Next take a step to the side, and pull your opponent along. At the same time, pull your opponent's neck with a jerk, and push the biceps. Follow up with a powerful knee kick.

A–F: *The opponent tries to grab from below. Saiyok (right) defends his position by blocking his opponent's technique on the upper arm. He steps forward with his left leg, pulling along his right leg and his opponent. He then follows with a knee kick.*

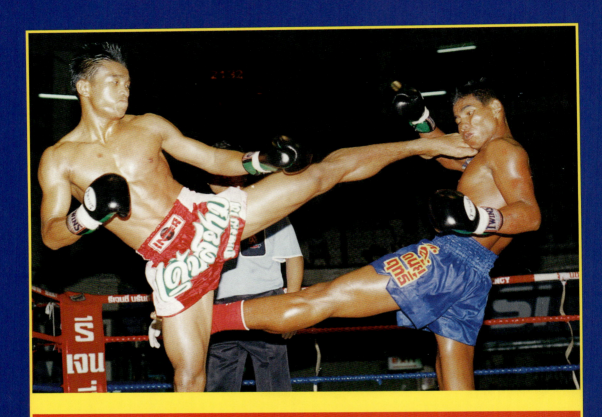

Densayarm Lukprabat strikes Fahpichit Sor Danairit with a round kick to the head.
The winner was Densayarm. Rajadamnern Stadium, Bangkok, 2000.

Chapter 9
Muay Thai Boran

1. Introduction

Big arenas were built in Thailand in the 1950s. A large number of spectators could now attend Muay Thai events, which resulted in large increases in prize money. Attracted by this source of income, trainers in Thailand changed their programs so that today, students are no longer trained comprehensively but are being prepared for fights in the shortest possible time. The athletes receive intensive training in some basic techniques until they can be carried out instinctively and with power. In the course of their athletic careers, the fighters learn some additional counter techniques that suit their fighting style. Furthermore, in principle anyone in Thailand can teach Muay Thai. With this background, historic techniques have been more and more forgotten. In recent years, however, public offices in Thailand have started to promote Muay Thai as part of Thai cultural heritage, which has helped spread the amateur sport, and the prominence and popularity of historic techniques is again on the increase. Meanwhile, historic techniques are used for product promotion, and sports magazines show them on a regular basis.

Historic techniques make it possible to defend and counter simultaneously. Advanced Muay Thai athletes like to use them in their fights as they are effective and frequently lead to an early end to the fight. Many of the techniques have been forgotten, but similarities between them and some counter techniques, as described in this book, can be detected. This indicates that a number of the techniques are still being taught in Thai gyms even though they no longer retain their original names.

The fighters Sakmongkol Sakchalee and Yordmongkon Sor Sermngam demonstrate the Chorakee Fad Hang technique at a Muay Thai show, Rangsit Stadium, Bangkok, Thailand, 2000.

Many publications depict historic techniques without any exact explanation. Frequently they are presented differently by different authors, and the names are translated. This is because precise historical data doesn't exist, and the authors are relying on different sources. Historic techniques are difficult to master, and their use entails the risk of injury, so you should not attempt to use every historic technique that you've heard of or read about. Instead, you must carry out a critical assessment and ask your teacher about the chance of success, as the danger of injury could be greater than the potential benefit. It would make sense for Thai public offices to clarify discrepancies with the introduction of a single program for all historic Muay Thai techniques.

In the following pages you will learn about techniques that are frequently described as the basis of Muay Thai techniques. These fifteen techniques include the previously taught basic maneuvers for defense against an opponent's attacking techniques and the respective counters. The Muay Thai techniques are described here in the way they are often taught today. However, many different versions exist due to the fact that Mae Mai techniques have no rigid rules but leave plenty of space for interpretation. It must also be kept in mind that in the past, fights were held without boxing gloves, so fighters had other ways to determine fights with their hands. The Hak Kor Erawan technique, meaning "breaking the elephant's neck," for example, is actually a technique to control the opponent's head and break the neck, hence the name.

Being a good fighter does not mean that you have to master all of the following techniques. Many of the current Thai champions are unable to apply many of them. It is enough to learn and use the techniques that are easily understood and correspond to your own talents. You should initially learn the basic techniques, and subsequently the counter techniques. Once you have mastered them, you can start learning the Mae Mai Muay Thai techniques, as their application is several times more difficult and requires skills in the basic techniques and counter tactics. You must be able to use these techniques instinctively before they can be used in a fight. The historic techniques can be used against attacks from the left and right side of the body. A precondition is that the opponent attacks with power.

Muay Thai Boran

Mae Mai Muay Thai

Mae Mai 1: Salab Fan Phla
(Cross-Stitch)

Mae Mai 2: Paksa Waeg Rang
(Bird Peeping through the Nest)

Mae Mai 3: Chawa Sad Hok
(Jawa Throws a Spear)

Mae Mai 4: Inao Tang Grid
(Inao Stabs with His Kris)

Mae Mai 5: Yok Khao Pra Sumeru
(Lifting Sumeru Mountain)

Mae Mai 6: Ta Then Kam Fa
(Old Man Holding a Melon)

Mae Mai 7: Mon Yan Lak
(Mon Supports a Pillar)

Mae Mai 8: Pak Luuk Toy
(Impaling the Stake)

Mae Mai 9: Chorake Fad Hang
(Crocodile Sweeps Its Tail)

Mae Mai 10: Hak Nguang Aiyara
(Break the Elephant's Tusks)

Mae Mai 11: Naka Bid Hang
(Serpent Twists Its Tail)

Mae Mai 12: Viroon Hok Glab
(Bird Somersaults)

Mae Mai 13: Dap Chawala
(Extinguish the Lamps)

Mae Mai 14: Khun Yak Chab Ling
(The Giant Catches the Monkey)

Mae Mai 15: Hak Kor Erawan
(Break the Elephant's Neck)

2. Mae Mai Muay Thai
Mae Mai 1: Salab Fan Phla

■ **Opponent's technique: rear straight punch, powerful front straight punch**

Execution

In this traditional technique, perform a half-circle step to the outside as defense against a powerful straight punch. In a conventional stance, change your stance with a step to the right; as a southpaw, to the left. In combination with the step, use your front hand to push away the upper arm and your rear hand to pull in the wrist. The technique can break your opponent's arm.

This is a basic technique for defense with a semicircle to the outside. Other attacking and follow-up techniques can also be learned.

A–E: *Taweesak (left) defends himself against a right straight punch by taking a forward step to the left. At the same time, he pushes away his opponent's upper arm and pulls in his lower arm. If his opponent punches with his left arm instead, Taweesak must move forward to the right and change his stance in the process.*

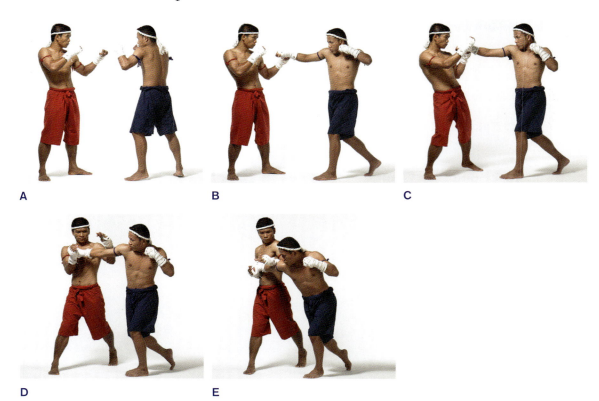

A B C

D E

Muay Thai Boran

Mae Mai 2: Paksa Waeg Rang

■ **Opponent's technique: rear straight punch, powerful front straight punch, swing**

Execution

The traditional technique is a defense against a punch by taking a step to the inside with a block so that you can then counter with an elbow. Take a step forward, turn your upper arm toward your opponent's punching arm, and block the strike with your opposite lower arm. From a conventional stance, change your stance along with the block of a left straight punch; southpaws when blocking a right straight punch. Follow up with an elbow technique, for which you can move ahead with your rear leg.

This is a basic technique for defense with a semicircle to the inside and a block. The block and the counter can therefore be taught somewhat differently. Some trainers, for example, teach the block against the punching arm with both lower arms. To this end, the hands are kept about eight inches apart, and the elbows approximately at shoulder width.

A–D: *The punch is blocked with the opposite arm, followed by an elbow counter. Taweesak moves slightly to the front for powerful execution. If his opponent hits with the left arm instead, Taweesak must block with his right arm and step forward with his right leg before he follows up with a left elbow to the head.*

A

B   C   D

Muay Thai Counter Techniques

Mae Mai 3: Chawa Sad Hok
■ **Opponent's technique: rear straight punch, powerful front straight punch**

Execution

In this traditional technique, defend against a straight punch by stepping to the outside, so that the punch misses its target and you are facing your opponent's back. Move the leg that's opposite the punch forward to the outside, and bend your body and head sideways so that you are outside your opponent's punching arm. Concurrently, hit with a side elbow to the body. The elbow can be delivered with your front or rear arm. You can also initially deflect your opponent's technique to the side, but this is not absolutely necessary.

A–D: *Taweesak defends himself against the left straight punch by stepping forward with his right leg to the right and delivering a lateral elbow. His striking arm is on the outside of the punching arm before he starts with the elbow technique.*

E: *The technique against a right straight punch.*

Muay Thai Boran 199

Mae Mai 4: Inao Tang Grid

■ **Opponent's technique: rear straight punch, powerful front straight punch**

Execution

In contrast to the previous technique, take a step forward to the inside in this traditional technique. In the process, bend your front knee and duck sideways with your body and head so that you are on the inside of your opponent's punching arm, which misses its target. Along with that move, deliver a side elbow to the ribs, stomach, or solar plexus. The elbow action can come from your front or rear elbow.

A–D: *Taweesak steps forward to the left with his front foot and delivers a side elbow from the inside. When starting his elbow technique, his head and striking arm are on the inside of his opponent's punching arm. The pictures indicate, however, that his elbow action comes a bit too early.*

E: *The technique against a right straight punch.*

Muay Thai Counter Techniques

Mae Mai 5: Yok Khao Pra Sumeru

■ **Opponent's technique: rear straight punch, powerful front straight punch**

Execution

In this traditional technique, defend yourself against a straight punch by bending your knees so that the punch ends up above your head. Follow up with a strike to the chin from a distance, for example with an uppercut; in the course of the action, slightly stretch your legs again for powerful delivery. The uppercut can be carried out with your front or rear arm. Some fighters bend the body laterally to the inside to avoid a deep bend.

A–D: *Taweesak defends himself against a straight punch with a deep bend. He promptly follows up with a powerful uppercut to the chin.*

E: *The counter with a rear uppercut.*

A B C

D E

Mae Mai 6: Ta Then Kam Fa

■ **Opponent's technique: rear straight punch**

Execution

This Mae Mai technique serves as defense against a straight punch with a block with the lower arms. Take a small step forward with the foot that's opposite the punch, and bend your knees. In addition, you can also lean back slightly to the side with the upper part of your body. In the course of the forward move, push your opponent's punch upward with your lower arm. Follow up with a powerful straight punch to the chin carried out with your other arm.

A–D: *Taweesak blocks a right straight punch upward. He moves slightly forward with his other foot and bends his knees prior to a powerful strike to the chin. Against a left straight punch, he would have to block with his right lower arm.*

A

B

C

D

Muay Thai Counter Techniques

Mae Mai 7: Mon Yan Lak

■ **Opponent's technique: rear straight punch, powerful front straight punch**

Execution

This traditional technique serves as defense against a powerful straight punch with a push kick. Deliver a rapid push kick to the chest, solar plexus, or stomach, and maintain a high guard with both arms. Pay attention to the use of the hips, and return your foot to the floor in front of you. Your opponent is put off-balance due to the kick and falls back. You can now deliver further techniques, for example a round kick with your other leg.

This defense can also be trained in for use against other attack techniques.

A–D: *Taweesak defends himself against a rear straight punch with a push kick to the stomach.*

A

B

C

D

Mae Mai 8: Pak Luuk Toy

■ **Opponent's technique: round kick to the body or head**

Execution

In this traditional technique, use an elbow as a direct counter against a round kick with the aim of injuring your opponent's kicking leg. Take a step away from the kick by moving forward to the outside with your outer foot. In a conventional stance, change your stance by taking a step to the right; southpaws by stepping to the left. In the move, turn toward the kick and deliver a powerful front elbow to the thigh. Be sure to protect your head with your other arm.

Some trainers teach this technique with delivery to the shin. This entails a higher risk of injury, however, due to the hardness of the shin.

A–D: *Taweesak defends himself against a right kick by stepping forward to the right with his right foot. In the process, he turns and delivers a right elbow to the thigh. If, however, his opponent kicks with the left leg instead, Taweesak must take a step forward to the left, turn to the right, and deliver a left elbow.*

A

B

C

D

Muay Thai Counter Techniques

Mae Mai 9: Chorake Fad Hang

■ **Opponent's technique: leaning back against a high round kick, rear straight punch**

Execution

This traditional technique becomes useful if your round kick misses your opponent. Continue your turn and deliver a spinning heel kick with your other leg. If your left kick misses the target, turn clockwise and follow up with a right heel kick. Having missed the target with a right kick, perform a counterclockwise turn.

As an alternative, you can return your leg swiftly back to the floor after the miss, and follow up from that position with a heel kick with the same leg to your opponent's head. The technique is also possible against a rear straight punch. Take a step to the outside so that the punch misses its target. Then deliver a kick with your inner leg to the unprotected side of the head.

A–D: *Taweesak's kick misses his opponent's head. He turns counterclockwise and follows up with a left heel kick from rotation.*

Mae Mai 10: Hak Nguang Aiyara
Opponent's technique: round kick to the body

Execution

In this traditional technique, catch a round kick and follow up with an elbow to the thigh to incapacitate the leg. Defend yourself by taking a step to the outside, away from the kick. In the process, catch the leg with your opposite arm and lift it slightly so that your opponent is put off-balance. In direct sequence, deliver an elbow from above with your other arm. In a simultaneous move, step forward with your leg on the same side of the body for powerful execution.

You can grab the leg from above or below. With the grip from below, it is easier to raise the leg. There is, however, the danger that it will slip along your arm and hit your face.

A–E: *Taweesak takes a step to the right while catching the round kick with a grip from below. He promptly follows up with a powerful elbow to the thigh.*

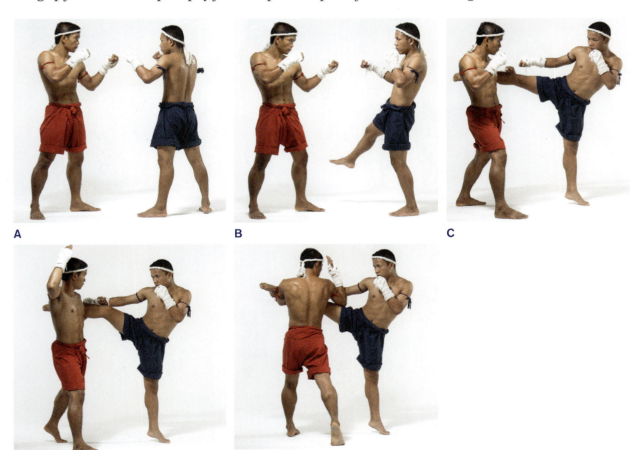

Muay Thai Counter Techniques

Mae Mai 11: Naka Bid Hang

Opponent's technique: push kick

Execution

In this traditional technique, catch a push kick, turn the foot to the outside, and deliver a knee kick. Take a step back when catching the push kick. Grab the heel from below with one hand, and put the other hand on the toes. Promptly turn the opponent's toes to the outside, and follow up with a knee kick to the calf, knee, or thigh.

Some trainers also teach catching the foot in a round kick with a subsequent upward turn of the foot. This is extremely difficult, however.

A–E: *Taweesak catches a right push kick, turns the foot to the outside, and follows up with a knee kick to the inside of the thigh. When catching a left push kick, Taweesak can move back with his left leg and follow up with a powerful knee kick with this leg.*

Mae Mai 12: Viroon Hok Glab

■ **Opponent's technique: round kick**

Execution

Employ this traditional technique by using a push kick as defense against a round kick. Kick with your heel or your whole foot to the groin or thigh. As a consequence, your opponent is put off-balance, and you can deliver a follow-up technique. A powerful push kick can even incapacitate your opponent.

Training in this traditional technique is usually that the technique is carried out with the leg on the same side as the opponent's kick.

A–D: *Taweesak defends himself against a round kick with a push kick to the thigh of his opponent's kicking leg.*

A

B

C

D

Muay Thai Counter Techniques

Mae Mai 13: Dap Chawala

■ **Opponent's technique: rear straight punch, powerful front straight punch**

Execution

This traditional technique serves as defense against a powerful straight punch by deflection and a technique of your own. Use your opposite arm to deflect the punching arm down to the inside. Concurrently you can lean your body slightly to the side. Follow promptly with a powerful straight punch with your other hand to the face or eye. If you block with your rear hand, you can step forward with your rear leg to facilitate the subsequent delivery of a powerful straight punch.

A–D: *Taweesak blocks the punch down to the right. He promptly follows with a rear straight punch. If his opponent hits with his left arm instead, Taweesak must block with his right hand while stepping forward with his right foot. He then counters with a left straight punch.*

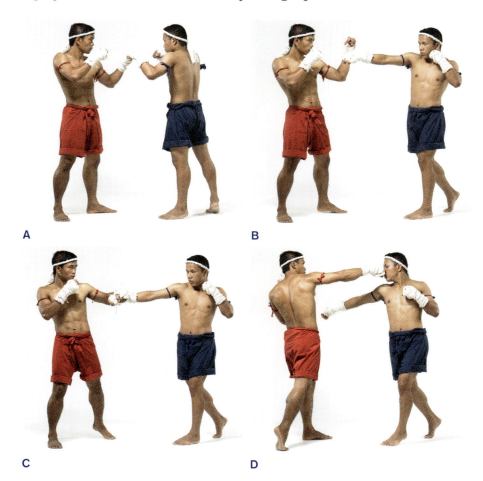

Mae Mai 14: Khun Yak Chab Ling

■ **Opponent's technique: attacking sequence comprising three techniques**

Execution

This traditional technique is learned for defense against punches, kicks, and strokes. In the basic technique, first block a straight punch to the outside. Then continue the defense with an elbow to the thigh. Finally, block your opponent's elbow technique. You are now in position to deliver your own attacking techniques.

Advanced athletes can vary their attacking techniques.

A–D: *Taweesak initially blocks a straight punch to the side. He then defends himself against a round kick with an elbow to the thigh. He finally blocks a rotating elbow and is now in a position to counter.*

A

B

C

D

Muay Thai Counter Techniques

Mae Mai 15: Hak Kor Erawan

■ **Opponent's technique: rear straight punch, powerful front straight punch**

Execution

In this traditional technique, a punch is deflected sideways, followed by controlling your opponent by the neck and achieving a knockout with a powerful knee kick. Block the punch down to the outside with your opposite lower arm. Use your other hand to grab promptly around your opponent's neck. Next pull your opponent's head toward you and follow with a knee kick to the head, solar plexus, or stomach.

The technique can also be applied against swings or a side hook.

A–D: *Taweesak blocks the punch to the outside, pulls the opponent toward him with the other hand, and follows with a rear knee kick.*

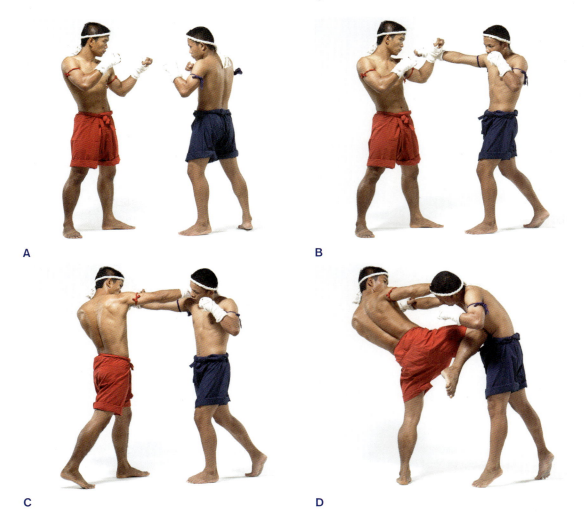

Manja Kietnapachai hits Singdum Or Aukrit with a round kick to the head.
Lumpinee Stadium, Bangkok, 1999.

Chapter 10
Training in Thailand

1. Frequently Asked Questions

Athletes with an intense interest in Muay Thai frequently want to experience this martial art in its country of origin. In Thailand it is possible to watch the best international Thai boxers in training and in actual competitions and have the opportunity to substantially improve your performance level due to the excellent trainers and training partners. In addition, training and recreation can be combined in Thailand, a vacation paradise.

Training in Thailand can also be recommended to Muay Thai practitioners who don't have the chance to spar in their local environments. After an intensive course in Thailand, training can be continued at home, or it may even be possible to offer Thai boxing courses.

I took the opportunity to travel to Thailand as a novice in Muay Thai and to learn the techniques thoroughly there. To achieve my goal I trained for several months each year at professional martial arts gyms

Christoph and other boxers during training at Fairtex Gym, Bangkok, 2000.

over an extended period of time. I also managed a Muay Thai gym for a year in the south of Thailand. The questions I was asked most often about training in Thailand are outlined in this section, together with answers.

▰ Is Thailand dangerous, and what are the people like that you met in training?

Thailand is considered a fairly safe holiday destination. When you're not familiar with the place, you should avoid certain areas, especially at night. Also, it is better not to show off with money, which may invite theft. If you respect cultural differences and pay attention to the rules of conduct outlined below, you can experience a wonderful journey. In the course of my frequent travels to Thailand, I have never been robbed and have never observed any incident of the kind.

Muay Thai training is done by a wide variety of people. You might meet Australian lifeguards, soldiers, or Ivy League students. One athlete might be trying to make money on the professional Thai boxing circuit, while others are enjoying an extended vacation. Many of those interested in training in Muay Thai are doing so with the idea of opening their own martial arts studios. This demonstrates that Muay Thai training is not limited to certain types of people. Training in Thailand is not reserved for specific groups of people but can be enjoyed by anyone, provided you select a gym tailored to your requirements.

▰ Are women allowed to participate in training, and are there age restrictions?

Fights between women are becoming more popular in Thailand, and a large number of gyms have become available to women. But depending on the priorities of the gym, not all training facilities accept the participation of women.

There is no age restriction for participating in training. Children may also train in some gyms. Parents should observe the training, however, at least for the first few days. If you are traveling on your own, you have to be at least age eighteen; otherwise no age restrictions exist. It is recommended, however, that individuals of advanced age select a gym with an international reputation, as they usually offer a higher level of comfort. Furthermore, gyms that are frequented by foreigners are better prepared to meet the desires and demands of foreign customers. To protect against the sun, the training site should have a roof. These days you can even find gyms where training is conducted completely indoors.

■ Isn't Thailand too hot for training?

The very hot part of the summer in Thailand runs from March to May. Allow ample time for your body to get acclimated to the local conditions. If your body gets used to the climate, even during the hot season, you can go ahead and start training. Your body requires a few days to adapt. For this reason, you should never start intensive training in the first few days after you arrive. The training units must end promptly, even though you may have the energy to continue. Overdoing it puts you in danger of falling ill, which could ruin your visit.

Be wary of air-conditioning. Athletes drenched in sweat who check into air-conditioned lodgings are very much at risk of catching a cold. The bigger gyms make it possible to train at different times of the day, so you can practice Muay Thai at a temperature best suited for you.

■ What health problems can be expected?

Diarrhea is the most frequent illness, which you can usually overcome in a short time. Hepatitis, rabies, and malaria, not usually well known in the West, are sporadically reported. In addition, be aware of the dangers of sexually transmitted diseases.

Thailand has poisonous and stinging animals. They rarely attack people, and even venomous snakes usually attack only in self-defense.

■ What prerequisites do I need for Muay Thai?

To be able to train in Thai gyms, you usually do not have to be in a particularly good physical shape, and comprehensive prior knowledge of Muay Thai is not required. It depends on the gym, however, whether you will be admitted. At some gyms, for example, there is a small group of highly skilled fighters, while other gyms are open to anyone interested in Muay Thai.

You can also start your training in Muay Thai in Thailand as an absolute beginner. To this end, however, you should plan for a stay of several weeks and not give up after initial minor difficulties. If you want to train with the same intensity as professional Thai boxers, you must

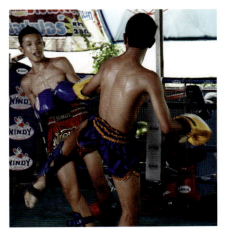

be used to regular training and have a comprehensive knowledge of Muay Thai.

▰ Do I have to be able to speak Thai?

In Thailand's tourist centers and major cities, you can get by with English. In rural areas you need a little Thai or to have dictionaries with you. In the course of an extended stay in Thailand, you will be able to pick up some Thai phrases fairly quickly.

In training, what you have to do is usually demonstrated, so you don't have to understand the language. In addition, trainers who instruct international students on a regular basis speak at least some English.

▰ How long should I stay?

The determining factors when planning your visit are your own expectations and goals. As a beginner, it is safe to assume you can learn the basic techniques after one month of daily training sessions. For advanced athletes, a minimum of fourteen days should be planned, which will allow sufficient time for your body to get used to the climate and to have a minimum of ten days of training at full intensity.

Trainer Oliver Glatow and Christoph, Muay Thai Institute, Rangsit, Thailand, 2000.

If your goal is not necessarily to improve your athletic performance, you can plan the visit for as long as you like. Fights can be seen in the tourist centers at regular intervals, and trainers can easily be found for individual training sessions.

▰ Where can I train, and how can I book the training?

Training facilities are available in all cities and tourist centers as well as in many villages. It is best to ask for a gym near where you're staying and to follow up with a visit to the gym. If you would like to train in a rural area, it is recommended that you visit one of the major arenas and speak to one of the trainers.

A stay at one of the major gyms can be booked via the internet. This is recommended as a first step for beginners. You should not book for an extended period of time because you will meet many trainers from different gyms on-site.

■ How is training structured?

The training in professional Thai gyms starts early in the morning, with another training session in the afternoon to avoid the midday heat. From Monday to Saturday, professional athletes train twice a day at different levels of intensity. The training of professional fighters often lasts two to three hours in the morning and another two to four hours in the afternoon. To allow the body to recover, there is usually no training on Sunday.

Training for foreign athletes depends on the performance level, physical fitness, and objectives. For best results the duration and intensity of training should be agreed on with a qualified trainer. In this context it should be noted, though, that Thai trainers educated in the science of sport also want adequate remuneration.

Some Thai managers have started to pay attention to the training of very successful fighters in accordance with the latest findings in the science of sports so as to develop the greatest possible performance level. This, however, is not yet the rule for professional Thai fighters as some managers and athletes lack the knowledge and understanding of training methods.

■ What is life in a gym like?

Thai fighters usually live at a gym. The overnight accommodations are located close to the training areas. They eat breakfast, lunch, and dinner together and also spent their free time together between the training sessions in the morning and late afternoon. Because of the hard training, it is a usual practice to take a rest at midday.

Foreign athletes usually have a hotel room or apartment of their own. A few athletes adopt the Spartan life of the Thai fighters, however, and cohabitate with the Thais in their shared accommodations.

In some Thai gyms, the cohabitation, meals, and even the training sessions of foreign and Thai athletes are separate. The Thai athletes in these gyms will be happy if you participate in joint activities, however. Spend as much time as possible with the Thai athletes, as this will give you a better insight into Muay Thai.

■ What is the best preparation for training?

You will achieve the best results from your training if you arrive in Thailand after proper physical preparation. If you are in good physical shape, you will perceive the training as less severe, and your recovery will be faster.

If your objective for the trip to Thailand is to improve your techniques and learn new techniques, you should concentrate on stamina training prior to your departure. Newcomers without previous experience in a Thai boxing club should have the greatest possible number of training sessions specific to the sport under the guidance of a teacher. For preparation, you should have a minimum of three weekly runs of between forty and sixty minutes. Additional training sessions are useful but are not absolutely necessary.

If your objective is very intensive and hard training in preparation for a competition in Thailand or at home, it is recommended that you prepare yourself with a balanced training program that contains components for stamina and power as well as training sessions specific to Muay Thai. Start training six times a week for four to six weeks prior to your departure, and alternate the sessions for stamina, power, and Muay Thai training.

■ How much does training in Thailand cost?

The cost of training varies widely. The same club may charge different fees for similar services, depending on how interested they are in an athlete. If they consider you to be a valuable future fighter for the gym, you can train for almost nothing.

International gyms offer fixed rates that can only be negotiated if you are planning to stay for an extended period of time. The total price for training, food, and lodging is about $30–40 per day. Some private trainers charge about $50 per hour.

If you look around locally, you will be able to find a trainer for about $5 per day. Thailand issues no training licenses to local trainers, so it is difficult to judge their skill level. Therefore, finding a trainer on your own can only be recommended to advanced athletes. Novices should first book a course in one of the known gyms and look for a better training environment thereafter.

There is, however, no guarantee of high-quality training at internationally known gyms, as the quality of training varies widely and depends on the trainer. You have the option to ask the management for a different trainer, however.

■ Where can I fight, and how can I become a professional fighter?

The most popular fight venues are in Bangkok. You will also find arenas in other big Thai towns and resorts. Some years ago, only top foreign athletes were allowed to compete in the big arenas. These days foreign fighters are particularly welcome in arenas with many foreign spectators.

All venues have different promoters who prepare a fight program with the aim of attracting the largest possible number of spectators to the arenas. Foreign visitors want to see more foreign fighters who are tall in stature, which is why the promoters are looking for these athletes, particularly at the holiday resorts. If you leave a good impression in training and are physically fit, you will be accosted regularly by promoters.

You must be very careful in the selection of your manager, particularly if you want to build up a long-term career in Thailand. Incident have been reported in which managers started to promote their athletes by picking easy opponents at the beginning, which resulted in increasing bets; the managers then used intermediaries to place bets against their athletes in later fights.

■ How much money can I earn in fights?

By Western standards, the prize money is very low. Depending on the arena and the opponent, foreign competitors start at about $50–150 for one fight. Big money can only be made with fights in Thailand if they are staged in big arenas and are shown live on TV. Acceptable prize money is currently being paid for fights in tournaments such as Thai Fight, the Toyota

Former WBC world champion Jaochalam Chatnakanok Gym.

Cup, and the Isuzu Cup. However, only a few foreigners are invited to compete in these events, which is why some athletes travel to Thailand to train but then compete in other countries. Even though Thai fighters can win purses of more than $10,000, it must be kept in mind that a big slice of it goes to the manager and the trainer, and that fights with this level of large prize are rare.

2. Travel Arrangements

General information

Thailand is part of Southeast Asia and covers a land mass of two hundred thousand square miles. To the west and north it borders Burma, to the northeast Laos, to the east Cambodia, and to the south Malaysia. The country can be divided in four climatic regions: the south with rain forests and palm beaches, the fertile central section, the mountainous and forested north, and the northeast with its rice fields. Thailand has a population of about sixty-seven million, of which about ten million live in Bangkok, the capital. The official language is Thai, but English is understood in the tourist centers and also in major cities.

The best time to visit is the fairly dry and cool period from November to February. The hottest period is from March to May, followed by the rainy season from June to October. Rainfall during the rainy season is usually limited to short showers, however, so it is also a reasonable time to visit. Detailed information can be obtained from Thai tourist offices or a travel agent.

The Thai currency is the baht; one U.S. dollar is worth roughly thirty baht. However, in the course of recent years the baht has been subject to sizeable fluctuations in its exchange rate. It is recommended to use traveler's checks or Visa or MasterCard credit cards, which are accepted nearly everywhere, making it unnecessary to carry large amounts of cash.

Visas

A visa is not required for visits to Thailand of up to thirty days. Your passport must be valid, however, for a minimum of six more months. For a tourist visa, valid for up to sixty days, or a nonimmigrant visa, contact a Thai consular office. This kind of visa can be extended if you leave Thailand via a land border crossing and return the next day.

If you want to stay for a period of six months, it is best to apply for a tourist visa that allows three reentries. After sixty days at most, you have to travel to a neighboring country and cross the border for a few hours. You can then return and spend another two months in Thailand.

A number of firms organize trips to the border for visa extensions. Such "visa runs" cost about $60.

After six months, you can apply for another tourist visa with multiple reentries at a Thai consular office abroad. This requires that you leave Thailand.

Thai Embassy and Consulates in the United States

Royal Thai Embassy
1024 Wisconsin Avenue NW
Washington, DC 20007
Tel. 202-944-3600
Fax 202-944-3611
consular@thaiembdc.org
www.thaiembdc.org

Royal Thai Consulate-General
700 North Rush Street
Chicago, IL 60611
Tel. 312-664-3129
Fax 312-664-3230
info@thaiconsulatechicago.org
www.thaiconsulatechicago.org

Royal Thai Consulate-General
351 East 52nd Street
New York, NY 10022
Tel. 212-754-1770
Fax 212-754-1907
info@thaiconsulnewyork.com
www.thaiconsulnewyork.com

Royal Thai Consulate-General
611 North Larchmont Boulevard, Second Floor
Los Angeles, CA 90004
Tel. 323-962-9574
Fax 323-962-2128
info@thaiconsulatela.org
www.thaiconsulatela.org

Thai Embassy in Canada

Royal Thai Embassy
180 Island Park Drive
Ottawa, ON K1Y 0A2
Tel. 613-722-4444
Fax 613-722-6624
consulat@thaiembassy.ca
www.thaiembassy.ca

Thai Embassy in Great Britain

Royal Thai Embassy
29–30 Queen's Gate
London SW7 5JB
Tel. 20-7589-2944, ext. 5500
Fax 20-7823-7492
csinfo@thaiembassyuk.org.uk
www.thaiembassyuk.org.uk

Travel Information

In the United States and Canada

Tourism Authority of Thailand
611 North Larchmont Boulevard, First Floor
Los Angeles, CA 90004
Tel. 323-461-9814
Fax 323-461-9834
tatla@ix.netcom.com, tatla@tat.or.th

Tourism Authority of Thailand
61 Broadway, Suite 2810
New York, NY 10006
Tel. 212-423-0433
Fax 212-269-2588
info@tatny.com, tatny@tat.or.th

In Great Britain and Ireland

Tourism Authority of Thailand
17–19 Cockspur Street, First Floor
Trafalgar Square
London SW1Y 5BL
Tel. 207-925-2511
Fax 207-925-2512
info@tourismthailand.co.uk, tatuk@tat.or.th

In Thailand

TAT Head Office
1600 New Phetburi Road
Makkasan, Ratchathevi
Bangkok 10400
Tel. 2-250-5500
www.tourismthailand.org
www.thailandtourismupdate.com/Home

Tourism Authority of Thailand (TAT) offices can also be found in all major tourist centers.

Vaccination

Approximately three months prior to your departure, it is recommended that you ask a doctor or a tropical travel clinic about what vaccinations are necessary.

Customs Regulations

Only one camera or video camera may be brought into Thailand, but this is rarely checked. You can bring up to one liter of duty-free alcohol as well as cigarettes and perfume for your personal requirements. When you plan to bring in medications, make sure their ingredients are not subject to the strict Thai drug laws.

The export of Buddhist statues that are too large to hand-carry is forbidden. Antiques may only be taken out of the country with a special permit.

Comprehensive information on Thai customs regulations is available at any Thai tourism offices.

What to Take

One set of business-casual clothing
If you visit a Thai government office, you must be dressed appropriately. This means sturdy shoes and long trousers, and a long shirt that covers your upper arms and chest. Business dress is also recommended for all official functions and events that you may be invited to. Otherwise, you only have to take the bare necessities, as clothing can be purchased in Thailand at good prices.

Diarrhea medication, insect repellents, and suntan lotion, prophylactic malaria medication
These items should be taken along as precautionary measures until you are properly acquainted with Thailand and its climate. Larger supplies are not required, as these products are readily available at the numerous Thai pharmacies.

Credit cards and American Express traveler's checks
Visa and MasterCard credit cards can be used at cash machines, in shops, and in hotels. These days overseas ATM cards are accepted by many cash machines. To prevent fraud with your cards, though, you should only use them at shops and hotels that seem reliable.

Cash machines have a tendency to be out of service for a number of days, so it is best to carry traveler's checks in addition to cards.

Important telephone numbers and addresses
Important telephone numbers and addresses that you should carry with you are those of your home country's embassy or consulate, the Thai tourist information head office, your travel agent, and the airline you used.

Copies of your passport and air tickets
You should have a copy of your passport, and keep it separate from the original. This will enable your embassy to issue a temporary passport without much delay if the original gets lost. If you lose your air ticket, you'll need a copy to show the airline.

It is recommended that you scan your ID documents and air ticket and email them, along with telephone numbers and addresses, to your own email account for easy and quick access.

Mouth guard

It is difficult to buy a mouth guard in Thailand as only few shops sell them. Some fighters don't wear a guard, but that is certainly not recommended due to the possibility of injury.

Important Addresses in Thailand

In case of emergency—if you are looking for an English-speaking doctor, or you have been robbed—you can contact your embassy.

U.S. Embassy Bangkok
95 Wireless Road
10330 Bangkok
Tel. 2-205-4000
www.facebook.com/usembassybkk
http://bangkok.usembassy.gov

Canadian Embassy Bangkok
15th Floor, Abdulrahmin Place
990 Rama IV Road
10500 Bangkok
Tel. 2-636-0540
bngkk@international.gc.ca

British Embassy Bangkok
14 Wireless Road, Lumpinee Pathumwan
10330 Bangkok
Tel. 2-305-8333
www.facebook.com/ukinthailand
http://ukinthailand.fco.gov.uk/en/

Medical Services

Thai practitioners are usually well educated. However, you have to pay the fees charged by private hospitals, which is why you should get health insurance coverage. Travel health insurance is usually offered by major insurance companies at reasonable cost.

To be able to claim medical costs from your insurance company, you have to get a receipt in English from the hospital for all the upfront payments you made. You also need a statement of diagnosis and the doctor's findings in English. All these records must be presented to your insurance company.

Precautions

Visitors to Thailand can easily contract mild stomach and intestinal illnesses at the beginning of a visit. These problems can usually be overcome quickly with common medication such as, for example, Immodium (loperamide). To avoid these maladies, don't buy food from street vendors on busy roads or from stands selling uncovered food. It is recommended that tap water be boiled before drinking, and don't use ice cubes or eat raw foods.

The question of whether a malaria prophylaxis is necessary depends on your destination. For most of Thailand, it is not required. A few weeks before departure, however, try to get advice on the current situation from a tropical disease clinic or the Thai Tourist Office. In any case, you should protect yourself against mosquito bites, which can lead to contracting dengue fever. Thailand has a large number of people infected with HIV. Protecting yourself is necessary for any sexual contact.

Bites by dogs, cats, or other warm-blooded animals entail the danger of contracting rabies. You should promptly seek medical attention, even if the wound is slight. If you are stung by a scorpion or bitten by a snake or spider, you should be able to describe the animal as clearly as possible so that a doctor can select the correct antivenin. To prevent this kind of injury, wear sturdy boots, especially in the rain forest.

The sale or possession of illicit drugs in Thailand has severe prison sentences and even the possibility of the death penalty. Prior to arrival or departure, pay close attention to your luggage. If you are not quite sure, check again. Never agree to carry a package from a stranger or a travel acquaintance.

Left to right: Christoph with Master Deycha and Taweesak Baoseehai, film stuntman and coach to film stars Jee Jaa and Osa Wang. Master Deycha, civil name Chitsanupong Nittayaros, was born 1960. He has had 145 professional fights and many more as an amateur. He studied sports and earned a degree in health and sport. He has trained many successful Thai fighters, including Terdkiat, and has trained fighters in Australia, Greece, Japan, the Philippines, Brunei, and Korea. See www.muaythai-muayboran.com.

Attacks on visitors to Thailand are rare. To lower the risk, don't visit desolate areas alone, and don't walk around unknown suburbs at night. To protect yourself from being mugged, avoid wearing valuable or flashy jewelry and showing off with money.

Hotel safes are normally quite secure. To avoid fraud with your credit cards, don't leave them behind when you're staying at a smaller hotel.

Conduct in Thailand

Interpersonal relationships in Thailand differ somewhat from those in the West. The following rules of conduct should be strictly adhered to.

- The royal family and monks are held in very high regard, and they should never be criticized or offended.
- Never touch the head of other people, including children. This is considered an insult, as Thais consider the head to be the seat of the soul. Also avoid touching casual acquaintances of the opposite sex; it would cause embarrassment for that person.
- Never raise your voice or show anger; such conduct is interpreted as weakness or loss of face. If you raise your voice or shout in a situation of conflict, you will make a fool of yourself. Speaking in a loud voice is generally considered impolite.
- Thais regard the feet as impure, and your feet must not be pointing in anyone's direction, must not be held high, and when you're seated, should not be aimed at the person in front of you. Also, don't step across individuals lying on the floor. When entering a temple or a household, remove your shoes. Avoid stepping on the threshold when entering a temple.
- Thais generally attach much importance to proper attire, and they dislike an untidy appearance. This applies to any place except the beach, and especially to contact with government officials or high-ranking individuals. If you don't pay attention to how you're dressed, you will be deemed antisocial and treated with disrespect.
- If you are greeted with a wai, you must acknowledge it with a wai. This exception is when dealing with beggars, who may consider it derisive.
- Generally speaking, you should treat the people politely and with respect. If they smile at you, reciprocate by smiling back. Behave in a friendly way so that minor mistakes in social interactions can easily be excused.

Training group with Terdkiat Sitteppitak (back row, second from left) inside the former Deycha Gym, Maha Sarakham, Thailand, 1998.

3. Selecting a Gym

The search for a trainer and a gym should be conducted with particular care, as the final choice will have a decisive influence on your athletic development. If you choose an unsuitable trainer for your goals, you waste time and will fail to make any rapid progress. If you plan a short visit to Thailand, it is recommended that you train at one of the internationally respected gyms. These gyms are accustomed to foreigners, the staff is able to communicate in English, and the athletes' requirements are known. However, the training fees are usually fairly high, and foreign and Thai boxers are frequently separated. A close relationship with the trainer, as is normally the case in Muay Thai, does not always develop. If you want to spend more time in Thailand for training, you should take a look at some of the gyms before you make a decision. You can also first train for some weeks in one of the better-known gyms before you look for a smaller and less expensive gym. You can avoid dissatisfaction by not booking a long training period in advance.

Gyms and a large number of trainers can be found in nearly all Thai villages and towns. To find a training gym, you can first decide on a town or neighborhood and then look for a suitable training facility in the area. Alternately, you can also go to boxing events, and if you like a fighter's techniques, ask his or trainer about the location of the club and whether you might be allowed to join. The comfort and equipment of these gyms are often not up to international standards, but it will give you the opportunity to gain inside knowledge of the sport, and the costs are considerably lower than at clubs with an international reputation.

If a manager sees a foreign athlete as a potential source of income, the athlete will only have to pay small or even no fees. Needless to say, you have to train hard enough at first to be accepted as an athlete by fighters and trainers alike. Some specialized gyms accept only a limited number of fighters for more intense training, and thus have a better chance to achieve a high ranking. Permission to train at one of these clubs is normally based on the current high standards in Muay Thai.

Additional details on Muay Thai can be found on the internet at www.muaythai.com, www.youtube.com/muaythaidvd, and www.facebook.com/muaythaibook.

A champion belt—the dream of every fighter.

Glossary

Following is a listing of the best-known basic Muay Thai techniques, listed in English with their Thai names. They are comprehensively described in my 2005 book *Muay Thai Basics*.

Fist Techniques

flying punch *(gra dod chock):* punch technique in the process of a jump

jab punch *(mat jab, mat throng chock num):* Straight punch technique with the front arm

overhead punch *(mat kong):* punch technique from above, similar to a crawl in swimming

rear straight punch *(mat throng, mat throng chock tam):* straight punch technique with the rear arm

side hook *(mat hook, mat weang sun):* lateral punch with the arm kept nearly parallel to the floor

spinning back fist *(mat weang glab):* punch technique in the process of a turn

swing *(mat weang yao, mat kwang):* lateral punch technique with a wide swinging motion

uppercut *(mat ngad, mat seri):* punch technique carried out from below with the arm held at an angle

Elbow Techniques

elbow from above *(sok sub):* elbow from far above, often in the process of a jump

flying elbow *(gra dod sok):* elbow technique in the process of a jump

reverse elbow *(sok kratung):* elbow to the back from below, often in the process of a turn

rotating elbow *(sok tee):* curving elbow technique through the opponent's guard

side elbow *(sok tad):* lateral elbow technique with the hitting arm held horizontally

spear elbow *(sok pung):* diagonal blow with the elbow from above, for which the elbow must first be raised slightly spinning elbow *(sok glab)*: elbow technique in the process of a turn

uppercut elbow *(sok ngad)*: elbow technique from below

Kicking Techniques

continued push kick *(te kod, na ca bid hang)*: semicircular kick slightly above the target, pulled down shortly before impact

half shin, half knee kick *(te khrueng khaeng khrueng khow)*: kick with the knee and the shin from a close distance

heel kick from above *(te kook)*: kick from above for which the leg is first pushed high in the air

high round kick *(te sung, te karn koa)*: semicircular kick to the head or shoulder

jumping round kick *(grad dod te)*: semicircular kick in the process of a jump

round kick to the body *(te lam toa, te tad glang)*: semicircular kick to the body, usually in the direction of the lower ribs

round kick to the leg *(te ka, te tad lang)*: semicircular kick to the inside or outside of the leg

spinning heel kick *(chorakee fard hang)*: circular kick from the outside with the heel, often in the process of a turn

Pushing Foot Techniques

back kick *(teeb glab lang, teep yan lang)*: kick to the back; the knee is first pulled in, which is followed by the leg to the target area

jumping front kick *(gra dod teep)*: straight push kick in the process of a jump

push kick *(teep trong)*: powerful forward kick with the entire foot or the heel

push kick to the leg *(teep robgaun)*: rapid kick, frequently to the legs to disturb the opponent's timing

side kick *(teep khang, teep sakad)*: lateral kick with the knee pulled in; in contrast to other types of martial arts, the body is not fully turned to the side.

Knee Techniques from a Distance

diagonal knee kick *(khow chiang)*: lateral knee kick, with or without grabbing

flying knee kick *(khow loy)*: straight knee kick in combination with a jump

knee bomb *(khow yon)*: straight knee kick in the process of a little jump

knee kick from above *(khow god)*: diagonal knee kick from above, for which the knee must first be raised

round knee kick *(khow khong)*: knee technique delivered in a circle from the outside

short knee kick *(khow noi)*: knee kick from a short distance to the thigh, to disturb the opponent's timing

straight knee kick *(khow trong)*: straight knee kick from a distance

Techniques in a Clinch Situation

grab knee *(jab koe tee khow)*: knee kick from the front or the side in combination with a hold of the opponent's neck

lock body knee *(goad aew tee khow)*: knee kick from the front or side in combination with a hold of the lower ribs

Bibliography

Cummings, Joe, Sandra Bao, Steven Martin, and China Williams. *Thailand Travel Guide*. 10th ed. Melbourne: Lonely Planet, 2003.

Delp, Christoph. *Das große Fitnessbuch*. Stuttgart: Pietsch Verlag, 2012.

———. *Dehnen für Kampfsportler*. Stuttgart: Pietsch Verlag, 2010.

———. *Fitness for Full-Contact Fighters*. Berkeley, CA: Blue Snake Books, 2006.

———. *Kampfsport Solotraining*. Stuttgart: Pietsch Verlag, 2009.

———. *Kickboxing: The Complete Guide*. Berkeley, CA: Blue Snake Books, 2006.

———. *Muay Thai Basics: Introductory Thai Boxing Techniques*. Berkeley, CA: Blue Snake Books, 2005.

———. *Muay Thai: Basic Techniques*. DVD. Lampertheim, Germany: Delp Sportverlag, 2011.

———. *Muay Thai: Counter against Elbow, Knee and Clinch Techniques*. DVD. Lampertheim, Germany: Delp Sportverlag, 2012.

———. *Muay Thai: Counter against Fist and Leg Techniques*. DVD. Lampertheim, Germany: Delp Sportverlag, 2012.

———. *Muay Thai: Training and Technique*. DVD. Lampertheim, Germany: Delp Sportverlag, 2012.

———. *Selbstverteidigung verständlich gemacht*. Munich: Copress Verlag, 2005.

———. *Thai-Boxen Fight*. Stuttgart: Pietsch Verlag, 2008.

———. *Thai-Boxen Training*. Stuttgart: Pietsch Verlag, 2012.

The Book Team

Sakda Neamhom

Fighting name: Saiyok Pumphanmuang/Windysport
Approximately 180 professional fights as of January 2012
Selected titles: WMC World Champion, Lumpinee Champion, Rajadamnern Champion, Channel TV3 Champion, Thailand Champion
Awards: Best Fighter 2010
www.muaythaiplaza2004.com

Buncha Chantawong

Fighting name: Sanghai MTP 2004
Approximately 80 professional fights as of January 2012
Selected titles: Isaan Champion
Fights in Hong Kong and France

Buncha Michaiyo

Fighting name: Danthai Windysport (MTP 2004)/Singmanassak
Approximately 190 professional fights as of January 2012
Selected titles: World Champion (WBC), Channel TV7 Champion
Fights in the Netherlands, England, and France

Chlame Boon

Fighting name: Saraya Nakhon Pathom Sport School
Approximately 50 professional fights as of January 2012

Kampan Santaweesuk

Fighting name: Rit KRS Gym
Approximately 100 professional fights as of January 2012
Selected titles: World Champion
Fights in Hong Kong and Australia

Taweesak Baoseehai

Fighting name: Petpatum Nakorntongparkview
Approximately 150 professional fights as of January 2012
Selected titles: South Thailand Champion
Coach of movie stars Jee Jaa and Osa Wang
Stuntman in action movies *Ong Bak 1* to *3, Chocolate*

Surasak Pakcotakang

Fighting name: Kem Sitsongpeenong
Approximately 140 professional fights as of January 2012
Selected titles: World Champion (WMC 154 IBS), two-time Thai Champion, Rajadamnern Champion, Thai Fight Champion
www.sitsongpeenong.com

Armin Matli

Fighting name: Armin Torprantaksin / Black Dragon Swiss
Approximately 70 professional fights as of January 2012
Selected titles: World Champion, two-time Thailand Champion
Fights worldwide

Nonsai Srisuk

Fighting name: Nonsai Sor Sanyakorn
Approximately 80 professional fights as of January 2012
Selected titles: WMC international Champion
Fights and holds seminars worldwide

Yuthana Pawanmata

Fighting name: Khumsap Kertnakornchol
Approximately 250 professional fights as of January 2012
Selected titles: Rajadamnern Champion
Fights in Hong Kong, China, and Australia

Yuthana Pawanmata (right).

About the Author
Christoph Delp

Christoph Delp is a martial artist, fitness trainer, and author of numerous books on martial arts and fitness, including *Muay Thai Basics, Kickboxing: The Complete Guide,* and *Fitness for Full-Contact Fighters.* His Muay Thai DVD series, designed to accompany his books, will be released in 2013. For more information, please visit:

    www.christophdelp.de
    www.youtube.com/muaythaidvd
    www.facebook.com/muaythaibook
    www.facebook.com/muaythaidvd

About the Photographer
Nopphadol Viwatkamolwat

Professional photographer since 1996
Brooks Institute of Photography, Santa Barbara, CA
www.astudioonline.com

Other Resources

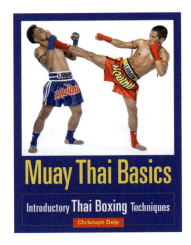

Muay Thai Basics: Introductory Thai Boxing Techniques

978-1-58394-140-9
$22.95
Blue Snake Books

In this hands-on guide to Muay Thai, renowned trainer Christoph Delp presents the sport's history, development, rules, and equipment. He explains basic skills, such as the correct starting position and footwork, and offers a complete list of all offensive techniques as well as a selection of effective defensive and counterattack strategies. The techniques are presented step-by-step by Thai champions from the famous Sor Vorapin gym in Bangkok, showing readers the fine details of each technique. The training section provides detailed information about the structure, content, and planning of training regimens; this includes historical training methods, a stretching program, and training schedules. Suitable as both a self-training guide and a supplement to club training, *Muay Thai Basics* offers authoritative instruction for Thai boxers and other martial arts enthusiasts.

Muay Thai Training Exercises: The Ultimate Guide to Fitness, Strength, and Cross-Training

978-1-58394-657-2
Blue Snake Books
Available in December 2013

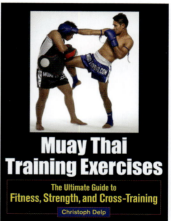

Effective martial arts training, especially for a demanding sport like Muay Thai, requires a prudent training plan. In *Muay Thai Training Exercises,* professional trainer Christoph Delp shows amateur as well as advanced fighters how to best utilize their training time, whether at home or in the gym, alone or with a partner or coach. A comprehensive guide for Muay Thai fighters as well as those utilizing Muay Thai techniques in Mixed Martial Arts (MMA), *Muay Thai Training Exercises* teaches effective exercises to improve flexibility, stamina, and strength as well as basic fighting techniques such as feints, counters, and combinations. Muay Thai champions Saiyok Pumphanmuang and Kem Sitsongpeening are featured, demonstrating their own training methods and most effective techniques. Training is broken down into core components that any Muay Thai fighter or instructor can use to help build an individual training plan; several ready-made, detailed training plans are also included for beginners, intermediate, and advanced practitioners. Rounded out with crucial information on nutrition, weight classes, and the importance of regeneration to effective training, *Muay Thai Training Exercises* will help all Muay Thai fighters to take their practice to the next level.

Fitness for Full-Contact Fighters: Training for Muay Thai, Karate, Kickboxing, and Taekwondo

978-1-58394-157-7
$26.95
Blue Snake Books

Physical fitness is an absolutely vital element for success in the martial arts. It is the only way to insure that powerful attacking techniques and rapid defense and counterattacking techniques can be employed over the full course of a competition. Martial artists require a special fitness training program that covers all aspects of physical performance.

In this book, author Christoph Delp presents a fitness training program tailored to the martial arts. The book details the basics of fitness training and offers an in-depth description of the various elements of fitness training: flexibility, stamina, and power. The exercises are presented step-by-step by leading martial artists. The book focuses on planning and monitoring training and presents complete training programs for newcomers as well as those at an advanced level. There is also advice about the correct diet for martial artists. This book is an indispensable guide for martial artists of all abilities and will help them to improve their ability to perform in training and competition.

Kickboxing: The Complete Guide to Conditioning, Technique, and Competition

978-1-58394-178-2
$26.95
Blue Snake Books

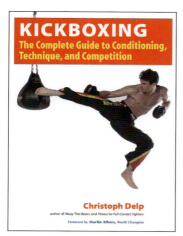

This comprehensive training manual features all the information needed for a successful start in kickboxing, right up to winning the match in the ring. Author Christoph Delp, an expert fitness coach and an experienced kickboxing and Muay Thai trainer, explains kickboxing's history, development, and rules as well as attacking techniques, defense techniques, and feinting skills. In spectactular photographs, champion kickboxers demonstrate these skills step by step, enabling the reader to easily duplicate the exercises and to understand their technical fine points. Chapters dedicated to training and competition contain vital information on training plans and structure, contest preparation, and competitive strategy. An ideal companion for beginners, the book is also an excellent reference for active kickboxers and other martial arts athletes who want to improve their techniques, either training on their own or as a complement to club training.

Illustration Credits

Pages 14, 16, 18, 19, 25, 29, 33, 41, 193, 198 (E), 199 (E), 213, 216 (B), 219 (B), 228, 229: photos by the author.
Page 11: Courtesy Lumpinee Stadium.
Pages ii, v, xx, 4, 6, 10, 15, 22, 23, 27, 31, 46, 47, 79, 129, 151, 192, 212: Courtesy Siam Sport Syndicate.
All other photos by Nopphadol Viwatkamolwat.